Indians and Archaeology of Missouri

Revised Edition

Carl H. Chapman and
Eleanor F. Chapman

University of Missouri Press
Columbia

University of Missouri Press, Columbia, Missouri 65201
Library of Congress Catalog Card Number 83-3596
Printed and bound in the United States of America

10 9 8 7 6 11 10 09 08 07

Library of Congress Cataloging-in-Publication Data

Chapman, Carl Haley, 1915–
Indians and archaeology of Missouri.

Includes bibliographies.
1. Indians of North America—Missouri—Antiquities.
2. Missouri—Antiquities. 3. Excavations (Archaeology)
—Missouri. I. Chapman, Eleanor F.,
joint author. II. Title.
F461.M79A8 [E78.M8] 977.8'01 83-3596

ISBN 978-0-8262-0401-1

∞™ This paper meets the requirements of the
American National Standard for Permanence of Paper
for Printed Library Materials, Z39.48, 1984.

Preface

There are many limitations and uncertainties in making a full interpretation of the archaeology of the state of Missouri, but we plan to go as far as we can to bring the past to life and to combine the various elements into a coherent picture of cultural development over the past twelve thousand years.

The goal of the book is to present specific archaeological knowledge in a form that is understandable, usable, and we hope interesting to the reader. We feel strongly that archaeology is of most value when the findings and interpretations reach the minds of the general public and become common knowledge.

We have based our interpretations upon research rather than upon imagination or speculation. Although our emphasis is on fact, it has been necessary to gloss over many problems and at times to oversimplify the sequence of events and cultures. In order to make a meaningful picture of the life of the time, we have extrapolated known modes of dress or usage into the past to fill out unknown aspects in need of description or illustration.

The work has been based on a background of actual experience with archaeological sites, materials, surveys, and excavations as well as on pertinent published materials. Although published references are not cited in the text, a selected reading list follows each section, and a glossary of specialized terms is provided at the back. A detailed bibliography on Missouri archaeology, containing the works from which much of the information in this book has been drawn, can be found in our *The Archaeology of Missouri* (2 vols.; Columbia: University of Missouri Press, 1975, 1980).

Unless otherwise specified, the drawings of chipped stone artifacts are two-thirds natural size. For all other artifacts, the largest dimension is given in inches to the nearest tenth.

We wish to express our appreciation to all those who aided us directly and indirectly in the project. Many of the illustrated items are in the Museum of Anthropology and the American Archaeology Division collections of the University of Missouri, the Missouri Archaeological Society, the Missouri Historical Society, the Academy of Science of

St. Louis Museum, the Illinois State Museum, and private collections. Our thanks go especially to Mr. and Mrs. Leo O. Anderson, Leonard W. Blake, Robert T. Bray, George Brooks, Mr. and Mrs. W. L. Brown, Richard S. Brownlee, Mary Bruno, Sadie Utz Clark, Mr. and Mrs. Harry L. Collins, Mr. and Mrs. J. M. Crick, S. P. Dalton, Mr. and Mrs. Walter M. Davis, Marilyn Powell Delling, Robert L. Elgin, J. Allen Eichenberger, Russell W. Graham, Mr. and Mrs. Henry W. Hamilton, Mr. and Mrs. T. M. Hamilton, Dale R. Henning, Sam C. Irvine, Walter E. Klippel, R. Bruce McMillan, J. J. McKinny, Richard A. Marshall, M. G. Mehl, Missouri Archaeological Society members, Missouri State Park Board, Rolland E. Pangborn, Gregory Perino, J. Mett Shippee, Frances Hurd Stadler, Francis L. Stubbs, John Taylor, P. F. Titterington, University of Missouri American Archaeology expedition members, Charles van Ravenswaay, Fred Winfrey, W. Raymond Wood, and Edward Zimmerman.

We are grateful to Mrs. John L. Funk for her helpful suggestions and to Mrs. Fred McKinney, Mrs. Richard Miller, Mr. Harvey Rathert, Mr. Donnie Wren, Mr. Harold Nichols, and the staff of the University Photo Service for their work on the production of the original publication, much of which has been included here.

Contents

Plains Indian War Club and Scalplock Rattle

Indians and Archaeology

In the Americas, Indians and archaeology are usually closely associated. The Indians found by the first European explorers were the culmination in culture and physical type of thousands of years of gradual change and development in both the North and South American continents. Wherever archaeologists investigate, they must work with the remains of the ancestors of the Indians if dealing with time periods prior to A.D. 1492.

There are several means by which the archaeologist can approach the problems of interpreting and explaining the evidences of the past when no written records exist. The main questions to be answered about the findings are *what* events took place that produced them and *where, when, how,* and *why* they occurred. Techniques and procedures for recovering the evidences are not enough to answer all the questions even though they are problem-oriented and rigorously scientific. Real progress has been made in answering the question of *what* by improved data processing, classification, and analysis; of *where* by new developments in surveying and excavation techniques; of *when* by the innovation of the methods of tree-ring dating (dendrochronology), radiocarbon dating, paleomagnetic dating, thermoluminescence, and others.

The questions of *how* and *why* the activities occurred that are reflected in the archaeological record are still a major concern that has not yet been solved satisfactorily. If the real world of personal relationships and interrelationships of the people who left the remains are to be interpreted and explained—the major goals of archaeological research—then carefully controlled theoretical constructs or models must be applied to the evidence. One of these, analogizing, is a type of reasoning that assumes that if two or more things agree with one another in some respects, such as similar form, they probably will agree in others. For instance, to help bring to life the activities of ancient Indians whose tools (Clovis Fluted points) were found with the bones of now-extinct mastodons in Mastodon State Park, the general knowledge derived from descriptions of big-game-hunting cultures throughout the world can be used. In like manner, the use of certain tools or weapons can be assumed by their similarity to those that have been observed in use by living groups of people. The closeness of fit of the archaeologists' findings to a particular model is one means of achieving the probability of the interpretation.

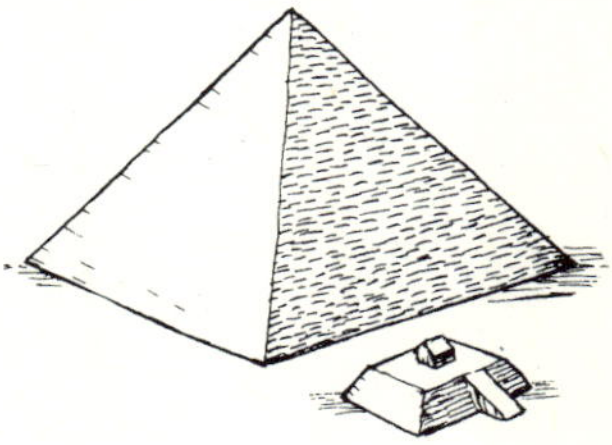

Analogy in itself is far from being the answer to the problem. When dealing with the past evidences of American Indians, specific information from American Indian cultures should be used whenever possible in order to increase the probabilities of accuracy. Thus, the archaeologist who studies prehistoric cultures in America must be a student of American Indian culture.

Mayan Glyphs

In preparation for the interpretation and explanation of archaeological remains, it is helpful to have a knowledge of cultures and cultural histories around the world in spite of the fact that there is only one general cultural development in the Americas, that of the American Indian. Parallel cultural developments did occur, and understanding the how and why of such developments can aid interpretations. However, we should not depend on far parts of the world to explain discoveries in archaeological sites in America. An attempt to use our knowledge of Egypt, Greece, or Babylon per se to interpret archaeological sites in Missouri is likely to be more confusing than enlightening. Comparisons based on general similarity of cultural development throughout the world can be misleading—for example, the equation of the pyramid-building Indians in the Mississippi Valley with the pyramid-building Egyptians of North Africa. The Egyptian culture had its roots in the Mediterranean general cultural evolution, whereas the Mississippi Valley development was based on the growth of culture in South and Central America, tempered by local innovations in North America. American Indian culture is a unique growth, with a historical background almost as ancient as that of Egypt, and it cannot be understood any more easily by knowing Egyptian prehistory than Egyptian culture can be understood by knowing American Indian prehistory; the two were totally separate. Thus, the best preparation for understanding and interpreting American archaeology necessarily lies in a knowledge of American Indians and of the long history of their development.

In the Old World the archaeologists who work with the classical cultures of Egypt, Greece, the Near East, and all later developments deriving from them must ally themselves with history for the interpretations of their findings. They work with cultures whose literacy extends so far into the past that historical records are available for their use.

Classical archaeology may require the knowledge of Greek, Latin, Egyptian hieroglyphics, or other special language tools. Classical archaeologist are often associated with art history, ancient history, and classical languages, and their background training is usually in those areas and in the humanities.

In the New World archaeologists are dealing primarily with the remains of nonliterate people. The Maya had writing, but the examples that have been translated, while fascinating, are of limited application because they are concerned mainly with astronomy, religious matters, and genealogies of rulers. Most American archaeologists are students of culture and behavioral science whose basic training is in anthropology, the study of physical and cultural mankind. They may utilize history, but the written records are limited primarily to only the few hundred years since 1492. There are specialists called ethnohistorians, who utilize both history and ethnology to study the Indians, and who are not necessarily archaeologists, and quite often archaeologists use ethnohistorical studies to interpret historic Indian sites. In fact, this approach is used so often that it is called the *direct historical approach.* The method is to start at the known historical period utilizing the known culture of a certain group, and then to work back to the unknown archaeological culture.

American archaeologists must prepare themselves with a broad background in anthropology, then use it to interpret units of culture obtained through archaeological research. The segments of culture may be from any time period, ranging from more than twelve thousand years ago to the era just prior to the coming of the Europeans to America.

When studies are made of archaeological cultures within a particular geographical region, the Indians who represent the peak of cultural development in that area are probably the best guides for the interpretation of the data. In America, Indians and archaeology are inseparable companions, and no matter how excellent one's techniques may be in archaeological excavations, no archaeological background is complete without a thorough grounding in American Indian ethnography.

American archaeologists are almost necessarily anthropologists with at least five years of college leading to a Master's degree and one or two years of practice under the direction of a competent professional archaeologist. This learning period should be comparable to that of a medical doctor in time and intensity. Most archaeologists undergo internship as well as instruction and hold a Doctor of Philosophy degree in anthropology. Thorough education and experience are necessary for the recognition and interpretation of the archaeological data when they are discovered as well as in the laboratory afterward. When an archaeological site is excavated it is destroyed, and the only evidences obtained are those recognized and recorded by the excavators. It is doubtful that you would let an untrained, unskilled individual who has done no more than read a book on surgery operate on you for removal of a gall bladder or an appendix. Yet untrained people often excavate important archaeological sites, thinking that they are producing valuable information. Actually, they are destroying irreplaceable information because they are not trained to recognize it or record it.

There are true amateur archaeologists who lack academic training but are capable of doing excellent archaeological work. These people are knowledgeable, and many are fully competent to conduct archaeological investigations in certain areas and specialties. Their instruction has usually been less intense and not so broad as that of the professional archaeologist upon whom they depend for the interpretation of their research; normally, much of their training has been guided by a professional.

Archaeology is not a treasure hunt—it is not a job to be done by Boy Scouts except under very strict direction and under the close supervision of a competent, fully qualified archaeologist. Our Indian cultural heritage is fast disappearing through the onslaught of progress in the form of dams, roads, other construction activities, and modern farming practices. Perhaps just as destructive is the thoughtless relic hunting by those who seek to satisfy their curiosity or their avarice. Relics from uncontrolled, random digging are out of context. They are almost completely valueless in determining the story they might have told if they had been properly recorded when in place.

Amateur archaeologists and others interested in learning about the past who make an archaeological discovery should report it to competent archaeologists for advice concerning further investigation. Such reporters often work with the specialist and thus gain experience and knowledge of methods and techniques. They are given credit for their discoveries and their work. Many amateurs have been honored by archaeological organizations for their accomplishments. For example, the Missouri Archaeological Society has presented achievement and honor awards to numerous individuals. Most states have state archaeologists, staff archaeologists within the office of the State Historic Preservation officer, or archaeologists with state or private universities that can be reached for advice or aid. In Missouri the place to report archaeological finds is the Archaeological Survey of Missouri, 15 Switzler Hall, University of Missouri, Columbia, Missouri, 65211.

Suggested Reading

Brennan, Louis A., 1973. *Beginner's Guide to Archaeology*. Stackpole Books, Harrisburg, Pennsylvania.

Fagan, Brian M., 1981. *In the Beginning: An Introduction to Archaeology*. Little, Brown and Company, Boston.

Hester, James J., 1976. *Introduction to Archaeology*. Holt, Rinehart and Winston, New York.

Hole, Frank, and Robert F. Heizer, 1973. *An Introduction to Prehistoric Archeology*. 3d ed. Holt, Rinehart and Winston, New York.

McGimsey, Charles R., III, 1972. *Public Archeology*. Seminar Press, New York.

McGimsey, Charles R., III, Hester Davis, and Carl Chapman, 1970. *These Are the Stewards of the Past*. University of Missouri Extension Division, Columbia, Missouri.

Patterson, Thomas C., 1973. *America's Past: A New World Archaeology*. Scott, Foresman and Company, Glenview, Illinois.

Sanders, William T., and Joseph Marino, 1970. *New World Prehistory: Archaeology of the American Indian*. Prentice-Hall, Englewood Cliffs, New Jersey.

Sharer, Robert J., and Wendy Ashmore, 1979. *Fundamentals of Archaeology*. Cummings, Menlo Park, California.

Our Heritage from the American Indian

Just what do we owe to the American Indians? All of us have heard of their importance in the early history of our country, but too often the Indians are placed in the role of villain. The fighting with the Indians in the Plains is too close to us, less than one hundred years ago, when the popular slogan was "The only good Indian is a dead Indian." The atrocity stories, companions of every war, and the propaganda used against the Indians have permeated our fiction, movies, and television. It is no wonder that this unjust picture has brought strong objections from the Indians and those knowledgeable about American history. Fortunately the true picture is beginning to emerge, which is that we owe a huge debt to our predecessors on the American continent. All of us enjoy untold benefits from things the Indians gave us.

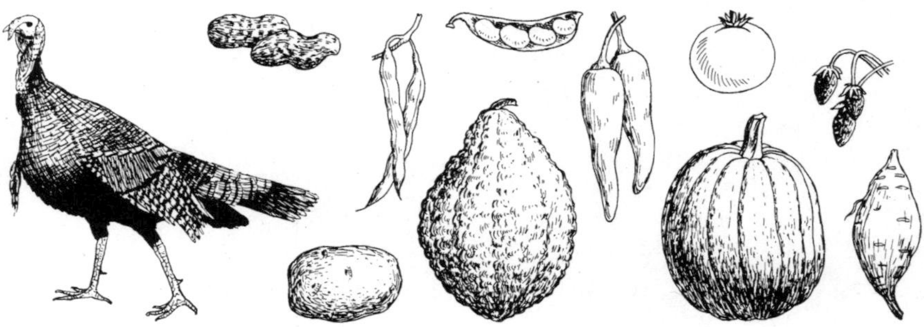

Can you imagine a Thanksgiving dinner without any of the following: turkey, Irish potatoes, sweet potatoes, pumpkins, and cranberries? These are some of the Indian foods we have borrowed.

The production of rubber from rubber trees is an outstanding contribution to our civilization. Who knows what the course of civilization might have been if the Indians had not discovered the production and use of rubber, quinine, and the coca leaf, from which cocaine is derived? They are Indian products of inestimable value to modern transportation and to our practice of medicine. The hammock, toboggan, and birchbark canoe were invented by the Indians before Columbus discovered America. The tale of Hiawatha is an Indian story that has become a part of our literature and has been read by innumerable schoolchildren. We have adopted the Indian game of lacrosse. Tobacco is now a part of American big business, and the Indian uses of tobacco—pipes, cigars, cigarettes, and snuff—have become an integral part of American custom. Our clothing has also been affected in such items as moccasins, fringed buckskin shirts, and parkas. Guinea pigs, which the Indians domesticated and ate, have been indispensable to medical research.

Remove the Indian names from our geography and huge gaps would appear. The states Alabama, Alaska, Arizona, Arkansas, Connecticut, the Dakotas, Idaho, Illinois, Iowa, Kansas, Kentucky, Massachusetts, Michigan, Minnesota, Mississippi, Missouri, Nebraska, Ohio, Oklahoma, Tennessee, Texas, Utah, Wisconsin, and Wyoming bear Indian names. Cities

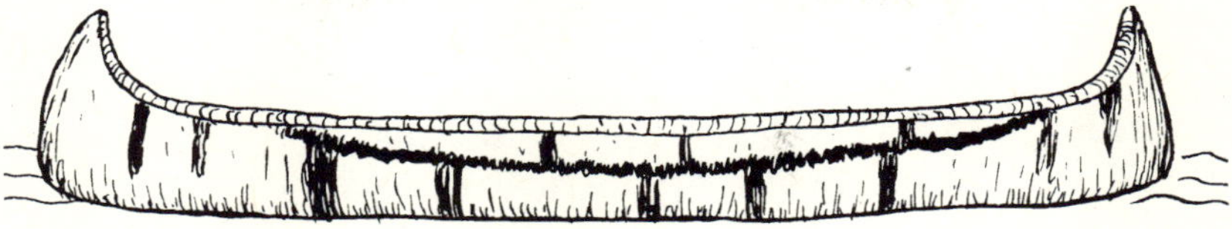

in every state trace their names to Indian origin, a few of which are Schenectady, Tallahassee, Mobile, Pontiac, Chicago, Kansas City, Cheyenne, Tucson, and Spokane. Here in Missouri the names of the towns and cities of Catawissa, Chilhowee, Chula, Kahoka, Kansas City, Miami, Monegaw Springs, Neosho, Niangua, Osceola, Pocahontas, Pontiac, Shawnee Mound, Spokane, Taos, Waco, Wappapello, and Wyaconda are Indian derived. Our Great Lakes Erie, Michigan, and Ontario, and our largest rivers, the Missouri, Mississippi, Ohio, and Arkansas, are called by Indian names. The Osage, Niangua, Meramec, Marmiton, and Wyaconda rivers are other examples of Indian waterway names in the state.

The Indian words *tomahawk, papoose, squaw, tipi, wampum,* and *wigwam,* along with many others, are commonly used in our language.

Indian arts and crafts are prominent as decorations in our homes or on our persons. Colorful Indian-made kachina dolls, pottery jars, ash trays, baskets, blankets, and rugs adorn many homes. Silver and turquoise jewelry, beaded belts, and moccasins add luster to the garb of the summer tourist or an exotic touch to usual wear. The Indian has definitely enriched the expression of our art in many forms.

The American Indian contributed many valuable things to our world culture. For example, more than half of the world's agricultural wealth today is estimated to derive from plants unknown to Europe and Asia before Columbus. To give the Indians the credit due them, a partial list of Indian contributions to modern American culture follows:

Food plants: Maize (corn), Irish potato (Peruvian potato), sweet potato, tomato, beans (lima, kidney, navy, pinto), chili pepper, pumpkin and squash, pineapple, strawberry, guava, peanut, alligator pear (avocado),

Lacrosse Racket

cashew nut, brazil nut, cacao (chocolate), manioc (tapioca), sunflower, "Jerusalem" artichoke
Prepared foods: cornbread, hominy (grits), "Hungarian" paprika, tamales, tortillas, popcorn, succotash
Fibers, gums, dyes, and drugs: long-staple cotton, agave fiber (sisal), henequen fiber, rubber, chicle (chewing gum), cochineal (dye), logwood (dye), coca (cocaine), chinchona (quinine), tobacco, curare, datura (pain reliever), cascara (laxative), balsams, ephedra (decongestant), pulque (maguey plant wine-distilled to make tequila), chicha (beer)
Clothing and adornment: parka, poncho, muff, moccasins, huraches (sandals), Panama hat (basketry hat), freshwater pearl beads, inlaid jewelry (turquoise, jet, shell), beaded belts, rubberized fabric (raincoat)
Domesticated animals: turkey, musk duck (Muscovy duck), guinea pig, llama, alpaca, dog breeds such as Mexican hairless, Chihuahua, Eskimo dog
Words: catalpa, cayuse, condor, conestoga, guano, jaguar, opossum, pampas, puma, raccoon, skunk, terrapin, totem
Geographical names: Keokuk, Milwaukee, Muskogee, Niagara, Omaha, Oshkosh, Ottawa, Pensacola, Peoria, Potomac, Saratoga, Sequoia, Susquehanna, Wabash, Walla Walla, Wichita
Miscellaneous items: cigar, cigarette, enema tube, hammock, handball, hockey, hollow rubber ball, kayak, lacrosse, maple sugar, marigold (domesticated flower), quonset hut, rubber, rubber syringe, snow goggles, tipi, tobacco pipe, tumpline.

All of these and many more have been taken from American Indians and used by us. It is easy to forget that it was the Indians who, over hundreds and thousands of years, domesticated, discovered, invented, or developed such important items as corn, chocolate, and rubber. If the Indians had not done so, we probably would not have the benefit of most of these things today. Our heritage from the Indians is interwoven thoroughly into modern American civilization; without the important Indian contributions the whole course of the development of the Americas and the world would have been different. Our lives would lack much of the enrichment we enjoy.

Indian Art in Shell from Missouri

Suggested Reading

Day, A. Grove, 1964. *The Sky Clears: Poetry of the American Indian.* University of Nebraska Press, Lincoln.

Driver, Harold E., 1961. *Indians of North America.* The University of Chicago Press, Chicago.

Edmunds, R. David, 1980. *American Indian Leaders.* University of Nebraska Press, Lincoln.

Hodge, Frederick Webb, ed., 1910. *Handbook of North American Indians.* 2 vols., Bureau of American Ethnology, Smithsonian Institution, Bulletin 30, Washington, D.C.

Josephy, Alvin M., Jr., ed., 1961. *The American Heritage Book of Indians.* American Heritage, New York.

Murdock, George Peter, and Timothy J. O'Leary, 1975. *Ethnographic Bibliography of North America.* 5 vols., Human Relations Area Files Press, New Haven.

Norbeck, Edward, and Claire R. Farrer, 1977. *Forms of Play of Native North Americans.* West Publishing Company, St. Paul.

Owen, Roger C., James J. F. Deetz, and Anthony D. Fisher, 1967. *The North American Indians: A Source Book.* The Macmillan Company, New York.

Spencer, Robert F., Jesse D. Jennings, et al., 1977. *The Native Americans.* 2d ed., Harper & Row, New York.

Steward, Julian, ed., 1946. *Handbook of South American Indians.* 7 vols., Bureau of American Ethnology, Smithsonian Institution, Bulletin 143, Washington, D.C.

Stirling, Matthew W., et al., 1955. *National Geographic on Indians of the Americas: A Color-Illustrated Record.* National Geographic Society, Washington, D.C.

Vanderwerth, W.C., compiler, 1975. *Indian Oratory.* Ballantine Books, New York.

Southwestern Indian Art

Indians of the Americas

When Columbus discovered the West Indies in 1492, he was not well enough versed in geography to realize that he had not sailed around the world, that the islands were not along the coast of Asia, and that the people were not inhabitants of the Indies, as eastern Asia was called in his day. No one else was any better informed, so when Columbus proclaimed the natives to be Indians, the name stuck. Today, notwithstanding a concerted effort several years ago to change it to *Amerind*, the name *Indian* has won out and is here to stay.

The Indians who met the early explorers and those who welcomed numerous other European visitors prominent in our histories put on their best red paint when they greeted the strangers. The use of red for face and body painting was such a common practice that the uninitiated Europeans came to the conclusion that American Indians had red skin. This fallacy persists today.

Nearly four hundred years after the first voyage of Columbus, some Indian groups still had never been seen by Europeans, or if they had, it was not recorded. It is not known how many Indian tribes or bands were in existence in A.D. 1500, before the European invasion of America, with its introduction of fatal epidemic diseases, began to change the tribal picture. Many tribes became extinct, while others banded together or absorbed neighboring tribes, so that the picture of native life in the Americas after 1500 was one of change. In spite of the changes, a major compilation on Indians in 1910 listed more than two thousand distinct Indian tribes or organizations in North America alone.

American Indians adapted to diverse environments in a wide variety of ways. There were hunters, fishers, and gatherers, but no two groups of people were exactly alike in regard to the things they hunted, fished, or gathered nor in the way they went about the business of gaining a living. There were horticulturists and livestock raisers, but the plants and the animals differed from place to place, and few Indian people depended upon a single occupation exclusively. The vast variety in the Indian cultures indicates a long time span during which the variations developed. Culture means the lifeways of the people, including the habits and customs associated with gaining their living, organizing their social and political activities, and practicing their religious rituals and ceremonies.

Indian tribes that were most alike in their habits, customs, and pursuits have been grouped in large geographical areas called *cultural areas.* A cultural area also has relatively uniform geography, topography, fauna, and flora within its boundaries. The Indians who lived in a particular area were limited in cultural development by their environment.

The physical characteristics of the Indians were almost as varied as their

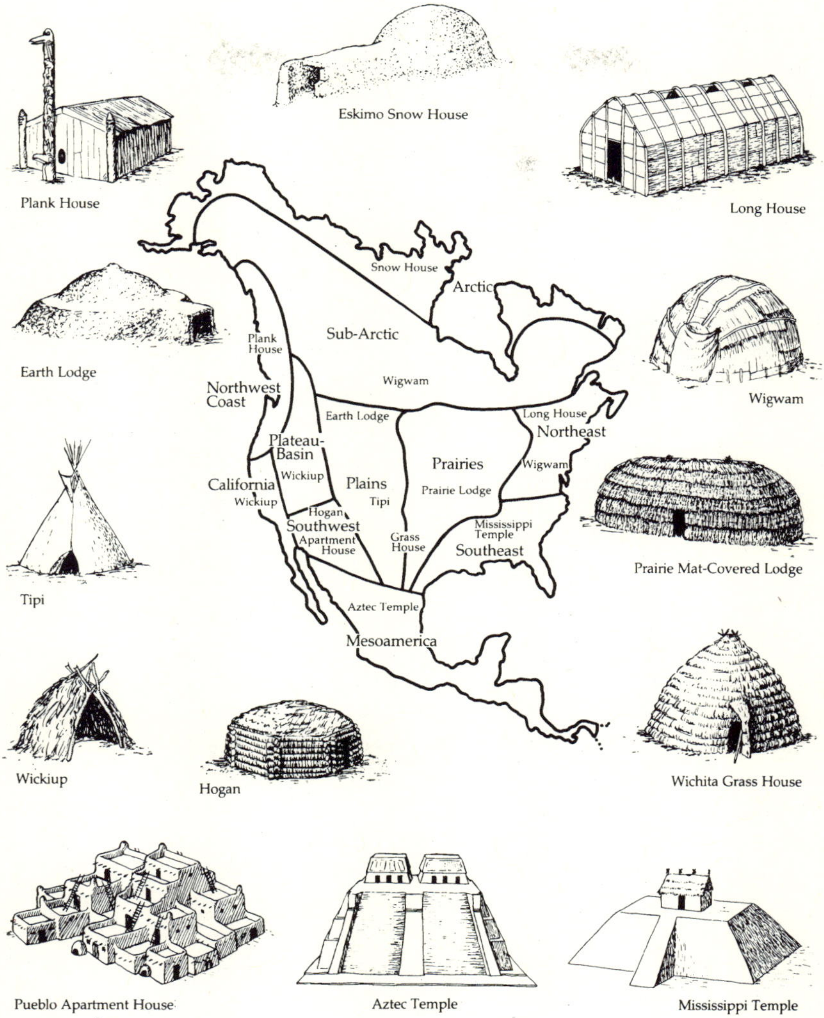

Cultural Areas: Typical Houses

cultures. Some were tall, over seven feet; a few were short, under five feet. Some had round heads, some long. Skin color ranged from a yellowish tan to very nearly chocolate brown. Noses varied from the small, short, snubbed nose of the Eskimo to the great beaked, Roman nose of the Plains Indian, so well known on the Indian-head nickel. Straight black hair, brown eyes, and high cheekbones were some of the universal characteristics. The exceptions were a few partial albinos who no doubt gave rise to the many stories of "white" Indians found in early accounts and used to support fantasies concerning the origin of the Indians.

Both cultural and physical characteristics point to a long span of comparative isolation from the Old World, in spite of the many interesting speculations to the contrary. There is no doubt that there were contacts from time to time, but the effects on the overall Indian cultures seem to have been negligible. Indian culture was developed by American Indians and was as distinct as that of the Europeans until the time of their discovery of the New World.

Indians today are remnants of the once populous and flourishing American people, and some of their colorful life can still be observed in twenty-two of the fifty United States. Missouri is not one of these, for soon after statehood all Indians were moved from her borders to the adjacent Indian Territory, later to become Kansas and Oklahoma. A Missourian who wishes to see Indians on reservations must go outside the state.

Most of the Indians, even those on reservations, are not very different from other Americans. They farm, raise livestock, participate in business; some are doctors, lawyers, or engineers, and many are in government work. There is no walk of life in which Indians have not taken part in the past or are not taking part at the present. Most of them live in houses much like those of the surrounding American communities. Occasionally, groups of Indians get together and participate in old-time ceremonies. War bonnets, skin clothing, beaded moccasins, and other heirlooms of the past are brought from storage and worn as symbols of the old life in which their grandparents and great-grandparents took part. Colorful clothing, songs, dances, and feasting hark back to former days and for a short time provide a glimpse into the past.

In certain places, nearly all in the Far West, the everyday life of Indians on reservations resembles that of the past. The Pueblos in New Mexico and Arizona are good examples. A current official highway map of those states will show the Pueblo villages and main highways leading to them. The Pueblo Indians have changed with the times, but enough of the old lifeways and forms of dress worn on special occasions remain to make a visit to the Pueblos like a visit to a foreign land. But it is not a foreign land—these people are Americans. They were here first. We are the foreigners. Their colorful villages, dances, pottery, rugs, jewelry, dolls, and baskets are more than just tourist attractions and collector's items; they are representations of a unique past that has modified our own way of life.

Suggested Reading

Axtell, James, 1981. *The European and the Indian: Essays in the Ethnohistory of Colonial North America.* Oxford University Press, New York.

Bahr, Howard M., Bruce A. Chadwick, and Robert C. Day, eds., 1972. *Native Americans Today: Sociological Perspectives.* Harper & Row, New York.

Boyer, Lee R., 1980. *U.S. Indians: A Brief History.* Advocate Publishing Group, Reynoldsburg, Ohio.

Castile, George Pierre, 1979. *North American Indians: An Introduction to the Chichimeca.* McGraw-Hill, New York.

Deloria, Vine, Jr., 1970. *We Talk, You Listen.* Dell, New York.

Denevan, William M., ed., 1976. *The Native Population of the Americas in 1492.* University of Wisconsin Press, Madison.

Edmunds, R. David, 1980. *American Indian Leaders: Studies in Diversity.* University of Nebraska Press, Lincoln.

Garbarino, Merwyn S., 1976. *Native American Heritage.* Little, Brown and Company, Boston.

Hertzberg, Hazel W., 1971. *The Search for an American Indian Identity: Modern Pan-Indian Movements.* Syracuse University Press, Syracuse, New York.

Hodge, William T., 1976. *A Bibliography of Contemporary North American Indians.* Interland, New York.

Hodge, William T., 1981. *The First Americans: Then and Now.* Holt, Rinehart and Winston, New York.

Josephy, Alvin M., Jr., 1968. *The Indian Heritage of America.* Alfred A. Knopf, New York.

Kehoe, Alice B., 1981. *North American Indians: A Comprehensive Account.* Prentice-Hall, Englewood Cliffs, New Jersey.

Laudin, Reginald, and Gladys Laudin, 1977. *Indian Dances of North America.* University of Oklahoma Press, Norman.

Leacock, Eleanor B., and Nancy O. Lurie, eds., 1971. *North American Indians in Historical Perspective.* Random House, New York.

Levine, Stuart, and Nancy O. Lurie, 1970. *The American Indian Today.* Penguin, Baltimore.

Nichols, Roger L., ed., 1981. *The American Indian Past and Present.* 2d ed., John Wiley and Sons, New York.

Oswalt, Wendell H., 1978. *This Land Was Theirs: A Study of North American Indians.* 3d ed., John Wiley and Sons, New York.

Smith, Jane F., and Robert M. Kvasnicka, eds., 1976. *Indian-White Relations: A Persistent Paradox.* Howard University Press, Washington, D.C.

Spicer, Edward H., 1969. *A Short History of the United States.* Van Nostrand Reinhold, New York.

Stewart, T. D., 1973. *The People of America.* Charles Scribner's Sons, New York.

Terrell, John Upton, and Donna M. Terrell, 1974. *Indian Women of the Western Morning*. Anchor Books, Garden City, New York.
Vecsey, Christopher, and Robert W. Venables, eds., 1980. *American Indian Environments: Ecological Issues in Native American History*. Syracuse University Press, Syracuse, New York.
Vogel, Virgil J., 1970. *American Indian Medicine*. University of Oklahoma Press, Norman.
Walker, Deward E., Jr., 1972. *The Emergent Native Americans*. Little, Brown and Company, Boston.
Wax, Murray L., 1971. *Indian Americans: Unity and Diversity*. Prentice-Hall, Inc., Englewood Cliffs, New Jersey.

Acoma Pueblo, New Mexico

Indians in Missouri

Missouri, due to its geographical location, has an exceptionally favored position in regard to the cultural areas in North America. The state lies in the heart of America's great waterway system. It is bounded in part by both the Missouri and Mississippi rivers; the Illinois and Ohio rivers meet the eastern edge and form a link to the Great Lakes and most of the eastern United States; tributaries of the Arkansas and the main stream of the White River help drain the southern boundary; there is access to the area from the

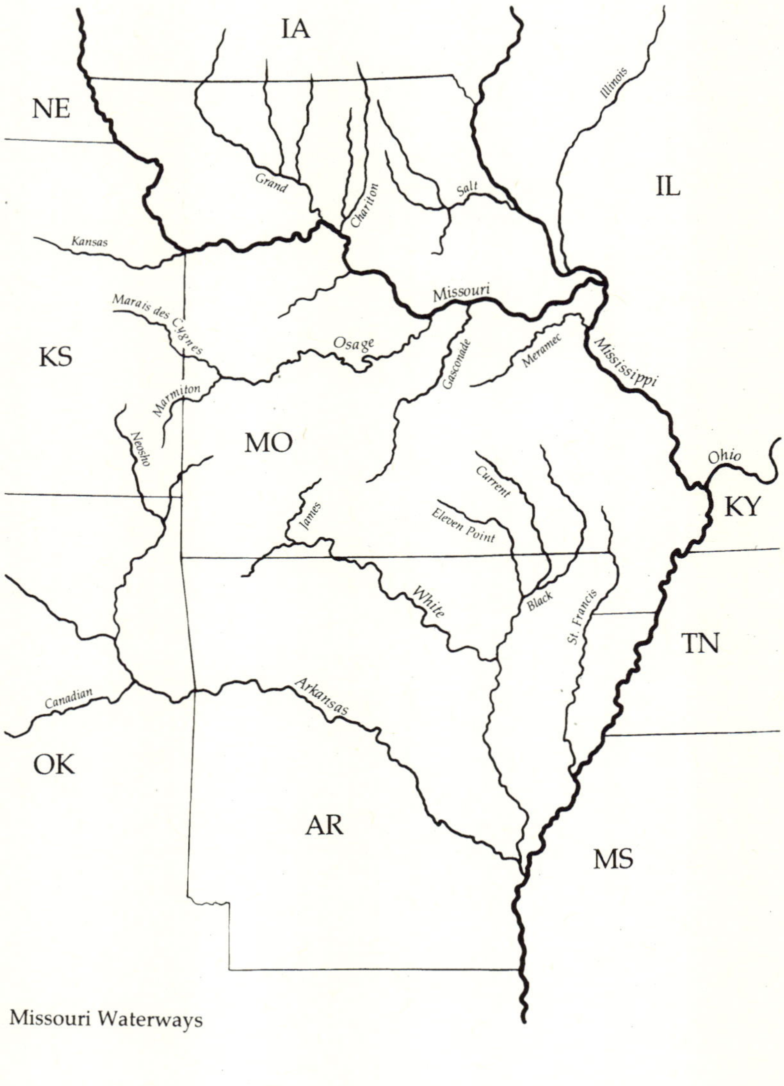

Missouri Waterways

north, east, south, and west by the largest streams in all of North America. Water-traveling Indians had routes to and from Missouri in any direction.

Water, the elixir of life, is never more than a short distance from any point in the state; thus the situation was always favorable for habitation. Furthermore, Missouri's location in the heart of the continent and at a latitude of vegetative change from north to south provides variety in animal and plant life. The change from grassland to woodland from west to east, due mainly to rainfall, further accentuates the variety of flora and fauna. Adding still more variety physiographically is the ancient uplift in the south central part known as the Ozark Highland. The state is bordered on the southeast by the riverine lowland, on the north by glaciated plain prairies, and on the west by prairies leading to the Great Plains. The physical, floral, and faunal diversity had their effect upon the life and customs of the people who developed there; the location overlapped the culture areas known as Northeast, Southeast, and Plains. Missouri was in the past, as it is now, a border state culturally and physiographically.

The Indian tribes native to Missouri in historic times were primarily the Osage and Missouri. The Kaskaskia, an Illinois tribe, lived on the west side of the Mississippi River from time to time, and there is some evidence that the Iowa and Kansas also had camps and perhaps villages in the area. Before 1800 Delaware and Shawnee moved to the west bank of the Mississippi near Cape Girardeau, and prior to 1825 there were Kickapoo, Delaware, and Shawnee reservations in the state. Other displaced eastern and southeastern tribes, including the Sauk and Fox, Miami, Piankashaw, and Wea, lived in Missouri for short periods.

The Osage Indian culture, although it has been very difficult to classify, can be considered representative of Indian culture in a border area. The center of Osage operations was in southwestern Missouri until the end of the nineteenth century. The people possessed numerous traits that would be classified as Plains, Northeast, and Southeast. Their cultural situation reflects the border position of the tribe both physiographically and culturally, for it demonstrates a blending of the surrounding cultural areas without any one becoming predominant. There are similarities to the Missouri tribe to the north, the Illinois tribes to the east, the Quapaw to the southeast, the Caddo to the southwest, the Kansas and Wichita to the west, and the Omaha, Pawnee, and Ponca to the northwest. The Osage were prairie dwellers, and their culture was adapted primarily to prairie living. Not until they moved from Missouri did they become more Plains-like, accounting for their inclusion as Plains tribes by some authors.

Missouri Indian Man (after Bodmer)

Suggested Reading

Foreman, Grant, 1936. *Indians & Pioneers: The Story of the American Southwest before 1830*. University of Oklahoma Press, Norman.

Ingenthron, Elmo, 1970. *Indians of the Ozark Plateau*. The School of the Ozarks Press, Point Lookout, Missouri.

Kroeber, A.L., 1947. *Cultural and Natural Areas of Native North America*. University of California Press, Berkeley.

Sturtevant, William C., ed., 1978–. *Handbook of North American Indians*. 20 vols., Smithsonian Institution, Government Printing Office, Washington, D.C. (See especially Volume 13, "Plains," and Volume 15, "Northeast.")

Swanton, John R., 1952. *Indian Tribes of North America*. Bureau of American Ethnology, Smithsonian Institution, Bulletin 145. U.S. Printing Office, Washington, D.C.

Tooker, Elizabeth, 1978. *The Indians of the Northeast: A Critical Bibliography*. Indiana University Press, Bloomington.

Osage Indian Woman and Child (after McKenney and Hall)

The Earliest Americans

The first people to discover America were the ancestors of our modern American Indians. The discovery was made before 20,000 B.C., at a time when mankind the world over was still primarily a hunter and gatherer. Some of the early explorers came on foot, carrying their meager belongings on their backs and in their hands. Others came by boat along the west coast, hunting and fishing as they gradually moved farther south following the sun. Those on foot walked across a land bridge that extended between Siberia and Alaska, marked by the Diomede Islands today. No matter whether they walked or boated, the groups could not have been large, consisting of a family or group of families numbering less than fifty and probably fewer than thirty individuals.

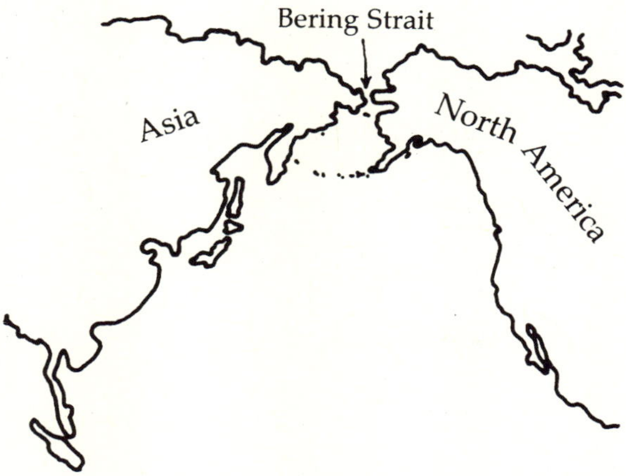

There was no fanfare, no one to greet them or to bar their way. The first people to set foot on the vast continent of North America were unaware of the historic significance of their move. If some day a monument should be erected to these first Americans, it would be similar to the monument of the Unknown Soldier of World War I in that the actual identity of the first discoverers of America will never be known.

Little absolute evidence of the first discovery of America exists, and where evidence is lacking or inconclusive, speculation enters. Explanations of the origin of the Indians have ranged from the prosaic to the fantastic, and some of the fantasies are to be seen in books and in feature articles and stories in newspapers and magazines. Fantasy and fiction have given way in recent years before the more considered theories of Indian origin and supporting evidence such as discoveries of weapons in association with extinct animal forms. Fiction purporting to explain the derivation of the Indians from such places as the continent of Atlantis, supposedly lost beneath the waves of the Atlantic Ocean, is given no credence today.

As yet there is no agreement as to the earliest evidences of human beings in America. It is known that more than twelve thousand years ago Indians were hunting the mammoth in what is now New Mexico, Arizona, and Mexico. Spear points of one group of early big-game hunters, found with the bones of the extinct elephants, have been called *Clovis* after the town of Clovis, New Mexico, near which the first finds were made. The Clovis points have grooves down the center and are called *Clovis Fluted.*

Another group of early men made a quite different type of spear point, named the *Sandia* because it was found in a cave in the Sandia Mountains of New Mexico. Sandia points are believed by some archaeologists to be as old as or even older than the Clovis Fluted. Sandia points are characterized by being inset or notched on one side only. Two types of Sandia points have been described, one lenticular in cross section and with pointed base, the other diamond shaped in cross section and with a straight or concave base that has been thinned.

Perhaps the best known of all the Early Hunter finds in North America is that of *Folsom* on a site near Folsom, New Mexico. Folsom dart points are fluted and are distinctive in workmanship. These points were first found at bison kill sites in association with *Bison antiquus,* an extinct form. Campsites of the early Folsom hunters have also been found. The Folsom people used choppers, knives, gravers, and scrapers of chipped stone, hammerstones, and rubbing stones. The fluted points were only part of a varied tool complex, but are the best known because of their distinctiveness.

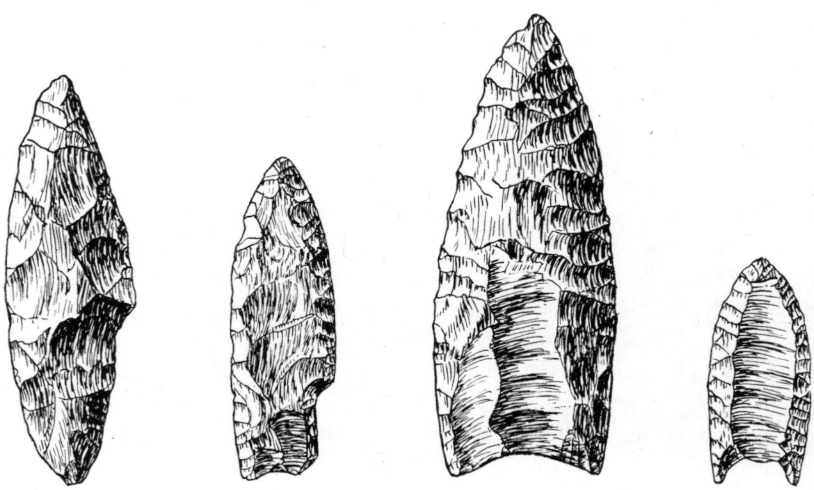

Sandia Clovis Fluted Folsom Fluted

Folsom people decorated themselves with stone beads and played with bone gaming disks. The women prepared animal skins with small stone scrapers and sewed with bone awls.

There were also several distinct groupings of early men that manufactured unfluted points of lanceolate shape. Spear point types representative of the different Early Hunter groups are the *Plainview* and *Browns Valley*. Other points made by people of equal antiquity are *Scottsbluff* and *Eden*. Characteristics often associated with the unfluted points are collateral flaking and diagonal ripple or transverse flaking, techniques of probable antiquity. The drawings show the characteristics of these early projectile point types.

Early Hunters were not just manufacturers of distinctive spear and knife blades, as might be inferred from reading archaeological reports. Their way of life is reflected in a variety of tools and industries. Although hunting was the primary way of gaining their living and big game was important, the large kills of mammoths by Clovis people represented by the Naco and Lehner finds in the Southwest must have been relatively unusual. In these instances, Clovis Fluted points were found associated with several mammoth skeletons. Early Hunters ate smaller game also, and grinding stones and hammerstones found on Folsom sites indicate that they ate seeds as well as meat. Spear points are important in identify-

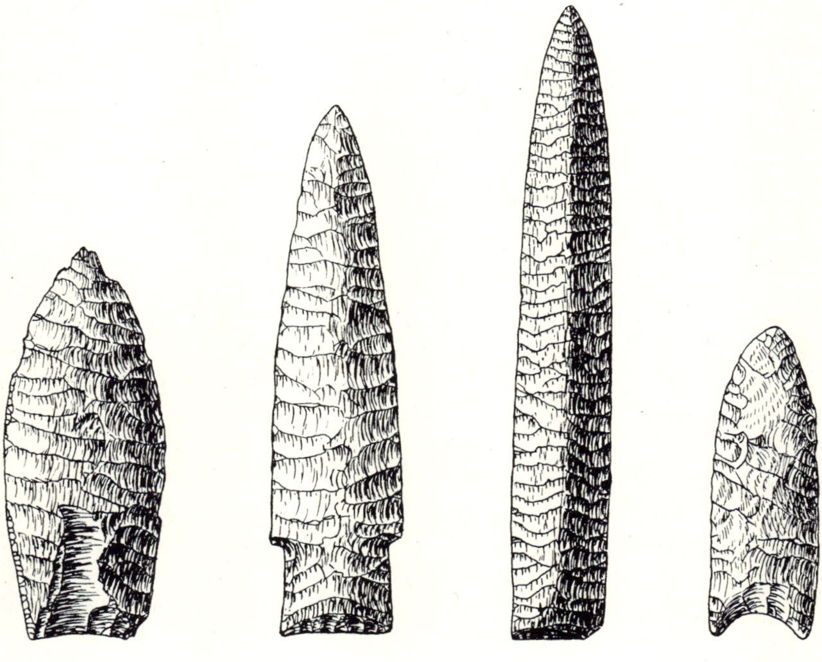

Browns Valley Scottsbluff Eden Plainview

Migration Routes
By Land and Sea

ing the Early Hunter sites, but the weapons are only a portion of the broader complex of tools indicative of the customs that made up the life of these early Americans. Stone flake scrapers and knives and bone spear points have been found on many Early Hunter sites.

Eleven thousand to eleven thousand five hundred years ago in what is now northern Mexico and the southwestern United States, the people lived in small bands and hunted camel, horse, mammoth, and giant ground sloth, large game that became extinct thousands of years before Columbus rediscovered America. Those people probably invented their distinctive spear points; there is no good evidence that they brought the idea with them or acquired it from elsewhere.

Perhaps the early hunters in the Southwest were remnants of an earlier, widespread cultural development that may have centered in the Missouri-

Mississippi Valley drainage area. Clovis Fluted points concentrate in that region, but have a wide distribution throughout the United States and extend as far east and north as Nova Scotia.

The migration routes that Early Man followed, whether on foot or by boat, may never be fully known. It does seem relatively certain that those in boats would have followed water courses of easy access and those on foot the areas of least topographical resistance, such as game trails. The migration route map presents several possibilities. The central regions, the well-watered Missouri-Mississippi drainage, was a logical region to attract and hold some of the wandering hunters and might well retain evidences of the early migrants to North America. The sufficient water supply and the variety of plants and animals must surely have been attractive to the early hunters.

Some researchers hold that the Americas were discovered and inhabited as long as fifty thousand years ago, while a few propose that the first settlers did not arrive until about twelve thousand years ago. Others have suggested that people came from Asia to America at a very early time, but that the mammoth and mastodon hunters did not arrive until about 10,000 B.C. Who is correct has yet to be determined, but the earlier estimates seem more plausible, and most archaeologists tend to accept thirty thousand or more years ago as probable for the time the first explorers from Asia discovered the American continent. The continued search for indisputable evidence of the earliest ancestors of the American Indians should eventually lead to one of the most exciting discoveries in modern archaeology.

Suggested Reading

Bryan, A. L., 1969. "Early Man in America and the Late Pleistocene Chronology of Western Canada and Alaska." *Current Anthropology* 10 (4): 339–65.

Butzer, Karl W., 1971. *Environment and Archaeology: An Ecological Approach to Prehistory.* Aldine, Chicago.

Chapman, Carl H., 1975. *Archaeology of Missouri, I.* University of Missouri Press, Columbia.

Claiborne, Robert, 1973. *The Emergence of Man: The First Americans.* Little, Brown and Company, Waltham, Massachusetts.

Haynes, Vance C., Jr., 1969. "The Earliest Americans." *Science* 166 (3906): 709–15.

Hopkins, David M., 1967. *The Bering Land Bridge.* Stanford University Press, Stanford, California.

Jennings, Jesse D., 1978. *Ancient Native Americans.* W. H. Freeman and Company, San Francisco.

Mason, Ronald J., 1962. "The Paleo-Indian Tradition in Eastern North America." *Current Anthropology* 3 (3): 227–78.

Reagan, Michael S., et al., 1978. "Flake Tools Stratified Below Paleo-Indian Artifacts." *Science* 200 (4346): 1272–75.

Scientific American, 1973. *Early Man in America: Readings from Scientific American*. W. H. Freeman and Company, San Francisco.

Ubelaker, Douglas, and Herman J. Viola, eds., 1982. *Plains Indian Studies: A Collection of Essays in Honor of John C. Ewers and Waldo R. Wedel*. Smithsonian Institution Press, Washington, D.C.

Wilmsen, Edwin N., 1973. *Lindenmeier: A Pleistocene Hunting Society*. Harper and Row, New York.

Wormington, H. M., 1957. *Ancient Man in North America*. 4th rev. ed., Denver Museum of Natural History, Denver.

The Early Hunters: Paleo-Indian Period

As early as 1838, only two years after Boucher de Perthes announced the startling discovery of man associated with "antediluvian beasts," Albrecht Koch found his mastodon and man in Missouri. Koch's description of his finds did not help get them accepted, for he reported that veins and tendons and other perishable parts were still preserved along with the bones. Such statements could not be authenticated or even supported by anyone else. Koch merely let his imagination transcend his actual data. This does not, as some seem to think, negate the authentic data he did describe. In fact, his data are more acceptable today than they were then, for there is not so much prejudice against them.

Koch's finds represent the earliest discovery of mankind in association with extinct animals in North America. The finds were made on the Bourbeuse and Pomme de Terre rivers and were described in much detail by Koch shortly thereafter. Unfortunately, the spear points found with the elephantlike bones were not described in enough detail to identify the types, and it has not been possible to equate them with any of the well-known Early Hunter spear points such as Clovis Fluted. At the Kimmswick site, where Koch also dug out mastodon bones, the association of Clovis Fluted points and mastodon and mylodon (giant ground sloth) bones has been verified recently. These discoveries at Mastodon State Park

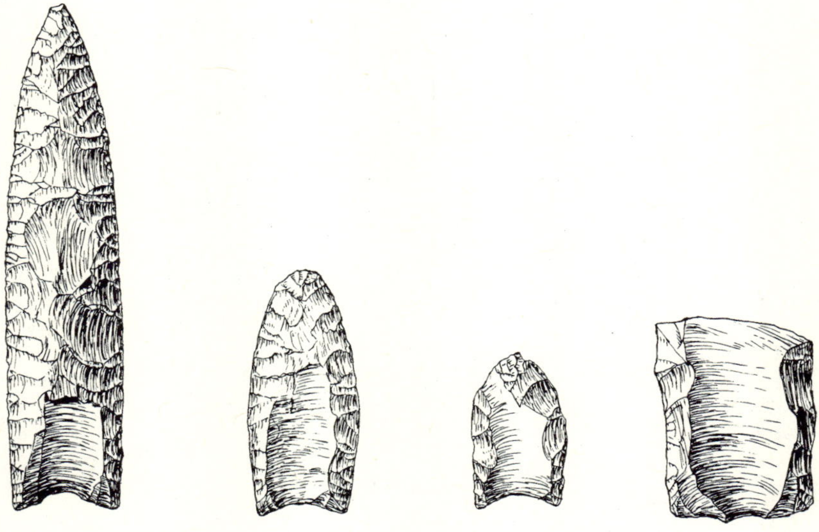

Three Clovis Fluted and one broken in manufacture (a reverse hinge fracture) from Mastodon State Park

by the Illinois State Museum vindicate Koch's claims whether or not he actually obtained the proof himself. A resharpened Clovis Fluted in contact with a mastodon rib bone and a Clovis Fluted broken by a reverse hinge fracture in the process of manufacture, found in the same area as a third Clovis Fluted, appear to be conclusive evidence that the early hunters camped at the site and were dining on mastodon and using sloth skins. Furthermore, the earlier find of a Clovis Fluted at the same site can now be accepted without question. All of these fluted points are shown in the accompanying drawings.

Giant Ground Sloth (*Mylodon*) (after Knight)

Prior to the Mastodon State Park excavations, the extensive distribution of fluted points throughout the Missouri-Mississippi Valley had been thought to indicate that the Early Hunters roamed the area. Furthermore, radiocarbon dates from some of the sites where fluted forms had been found were as early as those from mammoth "kill" sites in the Southwest dating in the period 9500–9000 B.C. At this time there is no question that the early hunters were in the central and eastern part of North America and were hunting the big game of the Pleistocene geologic period, the mastodon for meat and the giant ground sloth for skins.

It is now known that the fluted tradition of projectile point manufacture is represented by two different spear points, Clovis and Folsom. Clovis are earlier than Folsom and are the type found most frequently in Missouri and the eastern United States. Folsom are generally smaller, the flute extends the greater length of the point, and the flaking is more finely executed.

The origin of the specialized fluted form has not been determined. We propose that it was the Missouri-Mississippi Valley on the basis of the finding there of a greater quantity and variety of fluted forms. For example, the variations are great enough that a number of separate names have been proposed for them. A few are: Clovis Fluted, Folsom Fluted, Cumberland, Quad, Graham Cave Fluted, Ohio Fluted, and Enterline. They probably were invented by Indians in North America long after the first migrants arrived. As we have proposed, the variety of the fluted points, including Clovis and Folsom and related forms, in the lower Missouri–central Mississippi river region may indicate that this was the hearth of the development of the fluted tradition. The more finely ex-

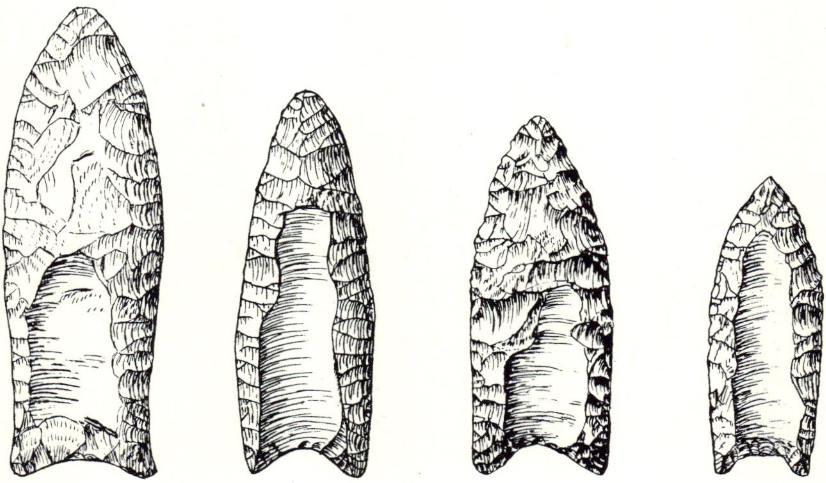

Clovis Fluted

Folsom Fluted

ecuted Folsom Fluted found in the Southwest and in Pennsylvania are later developments of the tradition, which spread almost equally from the center to the headwaters of the Missouri on the west and to the headwaters of the Ohio on the east. In any instance, the broad distribution of the distinctive fluted Clovis form in the central Missouri-Mississippi Valley is evidence that Early Hunters were living in the area much more than ten thousand years ago and were hunting the mastodon as demonstrated by the finds at Mastodon State Park. We still know little about the people who used the Clovis Fluted, and we know almost nothing about the people who preceded them.

Clovis Fluted forms have been found in Missouri wherever intensive archaeological work has been done. The Early Hunters who made them must have been limited in numbers and must have traveled far in search of game. At the time they lived, more than ten thousand years ago, giant beasts of the Pleistocene were still abundant and were hunted successfully. During part of the year the great valleys of the Missouri and Mississippi were choked with floods from heavy rainfall and the outwash of the melting glaciers to the north. Thus, much of the year the valleys were uninhabitable for both the hunters and the game they depended upon for food and clothing. Campsites of the early hunters have been found primarily at the edge of high prairies, which were the natural habitat of the plant-eating mammals that furnished most of the food supply. Campsites were never far from water, but water was more plentiful than it is now. The water table was high, and there were springs only a short distance from the hilltops. It is not surprising that the Early-Hunter campsite locations are often found today quite far from any source of water and on high areas away from the major stream system. The lowering of the water table has left the old camp locations high and dry.

During the Paleo-Indian period, 12,000–8000 B.C., great dust storms were common. As the glaciers melted and flooded the river valleys, the fine particles ground from the rocks carried by the glaciers were deposited in the flat flood plains of the major river valleys leading from the glaciated areas. When dried, the resultant powdery dust was picked up by gusty winds and redeposited on nearby river bluffs. At times the dust was carried miles beyond the river bluffs before deposition. Thus the early hunters had to contend with floods and dust storms; they moved frequently, and their tracks were literally covered with dust or washed away as they traveled.

Suggested Reading

Adams, Robert McCormick, 1949. "Archaeological Investigations in Jefferson County, Missouri." *The Missouri Archaeologist* 11(3–4): 1–72.

Adams, Robert McCormick, 1953. "The Kimmswick Bone Bed." *The Missouri Archaeologist* 15(4): 40–56.

Graham, R. W., et al., 1981. "Kimmswick: A Clovis-Mastodon Association in Eastern Missouri." *Science* 213(4512): 1115–17.

Griffin, James B., 1968. "Observation on Illinois Prehistory in Late Pleistocene and Early Recent Times." In Robert E. Bergstrom, ed., *A Symposium in Observance of the Centennial of the University of Illinois: The Quaternary of Illinois,* University of Illinois, Urbana.

Gross, Hugo, 1951. "Mastodon, Mammoth and Man in America." *Texas Archaeological and Paleontological Society Bulletin* 22:101–31.

Mehl, M. G., 1962. *Missouri's Ice Age Animals.* State of Missouri, Division of Geological Survey and Water Resources, Rolla, Missouri.

Wood, W. Raymond, and R. Bruce McMillan, 1976. *Prehistoric Man and His Environments: A Case Study in the Ozark Highlands.* Academic Press, New York.

Mammoth

Mastodon

(after Knight)

The Hunter-Foragers: Dalton Period

A problem discussed frequently by archaeologists is a means of separating the remains of the early hunters of the Paleo-Indian period from those of the foragers in the Archaic period. Some would separate the periods on the basis that early hunters specialized in hunting big game, the large Pleistocene animals that were extinct by Archaic times. Such a division would equate with the big-game hunters in the Old World in the Old Stone Age or Paleolithic period. It is a logical interpretation and tends to fit the evidence. In several places in North America there have been finds of spear points and cutting tools associated with mammoth, mastodon, giant ground sloth, horse, camel, and large bison, all of which became extinct at or near the close of the Pleistocene. Theoretically the problem is solved.

Unfortunately the early hunters left evidences more frequently at places other than the sites where they killed big game, and without the bones of the animals it is not really possible to determine whether they hunted the big animals intentionally and successfully or whether the kill sites that have been found were by chance and only an occasional rather than a regular activity. If the latter were the case, the term *Big-Game Hunters* would be misleading.

Whether or not the Early Hunter made a specialty of big-game hunting, they made specialized tool forms, the fluted points, that are so distinctive that they can be used to set them apart from Forager point forms. Again this does not solve the problem neatly because the change from the fluted points to other forms took place slowly over a period of about one thousand years. Here in Missouri, to account for the overlapping of cultural evidences this transition period has been named the Dalton period, and the culture typical of it has been called Hunter-Forager. The suggested time is 8000–7000 B.C.

Ten thousand years ago the last great Ice Age, which had reached its peak ten thousand years earlier, was coming to a close. Melting of the great ice sheets in the Great Lakes region continued to cause periodic and catastrophic floods in the Mississippi River and its northern and eastern tributaries. Subsequently the dust picked up on the river flood plains blanketed the land. Much of the big game, the mammoth and mastodon, were gone or had been reduced to endangered-species status. The people in the lower Missouri–central Mississippi valley were adjusting to a hunting-foraging economy in which small animals and plant seeds were prominent items of the diet. Fluted points were still being made, but the flutes were smaller and were not the most important distinguishing feature.

In the lower Missouri River Valley the less-well-made *Graham Cave Fluted* was present, and *Dalton Serrated*, a distinctive form with only minimal fluting, or basal thinning, was manufactured frequently. Much more im-

Graham Cave, a Registered National Historic Landmark in Graham Cave State Park

portant than the fashioning of tools was the fact that the hunter-gatherers were beginning to spend longer periods of time in a restricted area, supplementing their diet by collecting more of the edible plants found among the thick covering of vegetation in the valleys enriched by the glacial dust from the north.

The hunter-gatherers often sought caves and other natural shelters and one of them, Graham Cave, now in Graham Cave State Park, has yielded a limited picture of life of the people in Missouri during the Dalton period, 8000–7000 B.C. The wide-arched cave entrance, facing south, offered warmth and shelter. The fireplaces of the early people, the trash from food

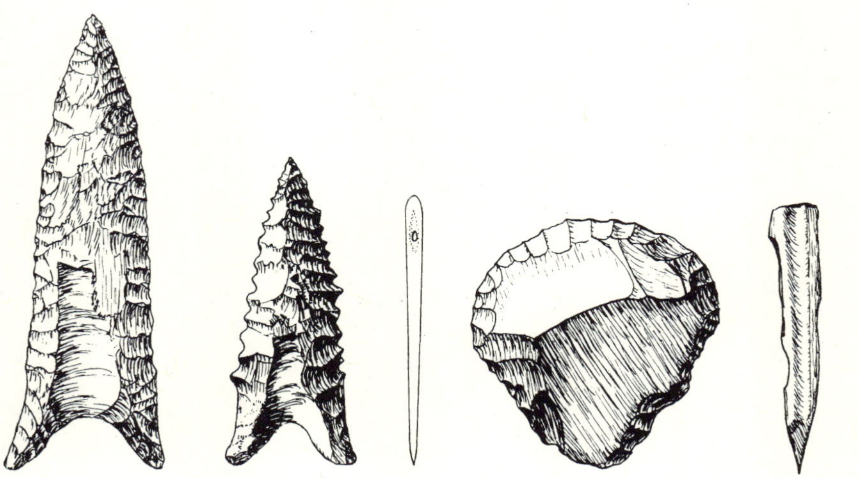

Graham Cave Fluted　Dalton Serrated　Bone Needle 2.1　Scraper　Bone Awl 2.1

preparation, lost tools, and other debris built up through living in the cave were covered by wind-blown soil. Deposits were also laid down when the Indians were not at home, for there is no doubt that the cave shelter was abandoned at certain periods of the year.

The finely made bone needles found in Graham Cave imply the making of fitted clothing to protect the hunter-foragers from cold winters. The small, eyed needles are similar to those used by the Eskimo and related groups who fashioned fitted clothing. Needles are required when tailored clothing is made; a simple awl is sufficient for sewing loosely fitted garments. Small flake scrapers are further evidence of skilled hide preparation. It is probable that the early women in Graham Cave were kept busy making clothes for the family as they sat around the fires on the floor of the cave.

Other products of the women's industry were handwoven nets for trapping small game and bags for collecting and storing seeds. The women may also have selected the stones on which they ground seeds and berries. Scrapers, knives, and drills were constructed from nodules of flint brought from the rock outcrops nearby, broken into manageable pieces, and then flaked into shape by the men.

Vegetable as well as animal products were important to the economy of the earliest inhabitants of Graham Cave. Seeds were ground on flat sandstone rocks selected for the purpose, or were crushed in mortars made by pecking out circular depressions in the flat stones. Cylindrical stone pestles shaped with rounded ends were used for pounding or crushing the seeds in the mortars, or like a rolling pin on the flat mealing stones. The women collected seeds, berries, and nuts and ground them into meal or

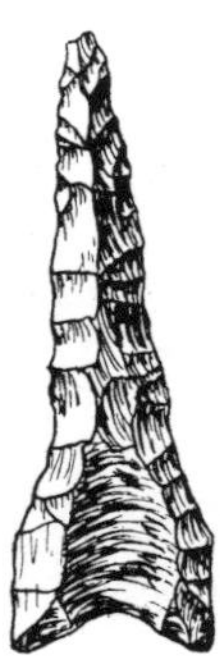

Drill 2.5

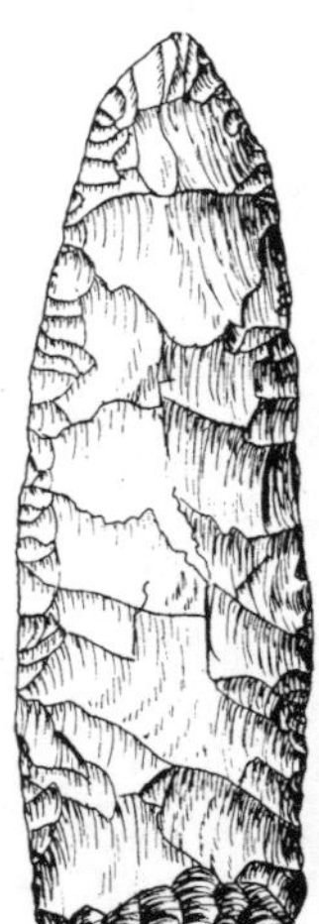

Knife 4.5

Adz 3.2

Mortar 9.4

flour. Edible roots also were probably gathered and dried for storage.

Among the tools found around the fireplaces in Graham Cave were adzes, spokeshaves, and steep-edged scraping and cutting tools denoting that woodworking was an important industry. Digging sticks to procure roots, shafts for spears, handles for stone implements, containers for food, and snares or traps were the items made of wood.

The earliest Indians living in Graham Cave spent most of their time hunting, gathering, and preparing food and making the tools and utensils necessary to obtain food and protect themselves from the elements. A little of their time was spent in ceremonial devotions; body and face painting probably was an important preparation for those who took part in rituals. Many cupstones full of red mineral paint and pieces of hematite paintstone that had been ground for powdered pigment have been found on the cave floor.

Ceremonies, perhaps shamanistic, are indicated by a ring of rocks encircling a large stone in one area of the cave. This area, interpreted as being a council ring or ceremonial area, is in the west corner of the cave. It may have been the local church or lodge of the earliest people using the cave. A large stone that originally had fallen from the roof had been utilized as a hearth for a small fire. Fire had been rekindled many times in the same place, for the stone was reddened and cracked. There were very few evidences of the usual kitchen refuse, suggesting that the area was used for ceremonial rites or councils rather than for domestic purposes.

The cave served occasionally as a burial place. One burial below the original floor of the cave gives an insight into the ceremonies associated

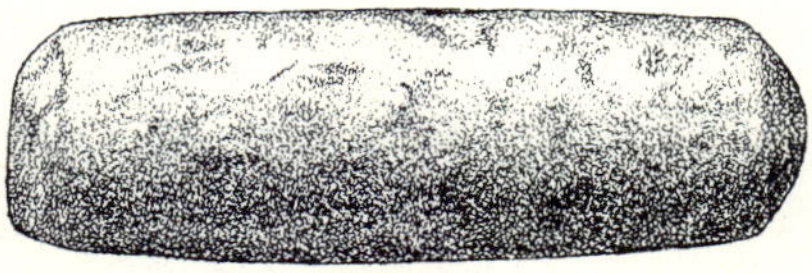

Roller Pestle 7.4

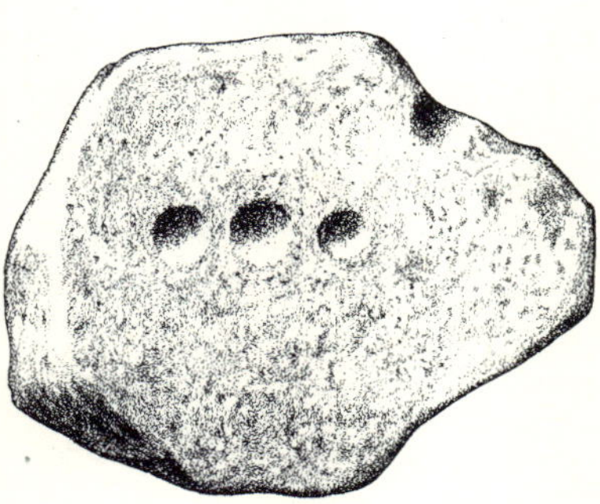

Cupstone 8

with death and the beliefs of life after death of the early Graham Cave people. That they cherished a belief in afterlife might be inferred from the funeral preparations. The burial was not in the flesh. No more than half of the larger bones of the skeleton were in the burial pit: the skull, collar bone, shoulder blade, half of the pelvis, a femur (upper leg), knee cap, tibia and fibula (lower leg), and a calcaneus (heel bone). These had been placed in approximate articulation in a semiflexed position.

A drilled coyote canine tooth found with the burial may denote that there was a mythology concerning the animal at a very early date. The coyote is an important character in Indian myth in historic times. In some stories Coyote is a trickster; in others he is a culture-hero and teaches useful crafts to mankind.

The Indian occupation of Graham Cave was intermittent, beginning about ten thousand years ago and continuing until about one thousand years ago.

The Dalton period sites in the lowland areas of southeastern Missouri and northeastern Arkansas are mostly small campsites that may represent the hunting headquarters of the Hunter-Forager people in that region. Their small size suggests that they were seasonal in use, and the association of many snubbed-end flake scrapers and flake knives used in preparing skins may further indicate their temporary use as hunting camps. Skin-working tools are always a part of hunting camp paraphernalia.

Logically these campsites would have been used as a winter station or base for hunting by the semisedentary hunting-foraging people. During the late spring and early fall the dense vegetation growth and the swampy flooded area would have made travel and hunting difficult. The same conditions, with the addition of myriads of biting insects, would have made the southeastern swamps less desirable as hunting places during the summer months. The most favorable time to hunt in the region would have been winter and early spring when vegetation was at a minimum. The small size of the campsites, their continuous distribution on most of the old natural terraces or levees, and the large quantities of camp refuse indicate a pattern of living on the sites for short periods and returning to the same places time and time again. Thus their wandering was restricted to a definite range. Hunts for certain game animals and trips to collect ripened vegetal foods must have limited the area in which the hunter-foragers of the Dalton period roamed.

Tool kits of the earliest hunter-foragers at Rodgers Shelter in southwestern Missouri denote that game, seeds, and vegetables were important food sources. Deer were prominent in the diet, and squirrel and cottontail also were valued. The terrace in front of the shelter was occupied intermittently by a small group of people, similar to the pattern at Graham Cave, but at Rodgers the first evidences had been buried by more than twenty-five feet of waterborne deposits, compared to the six feet of windblown soil at

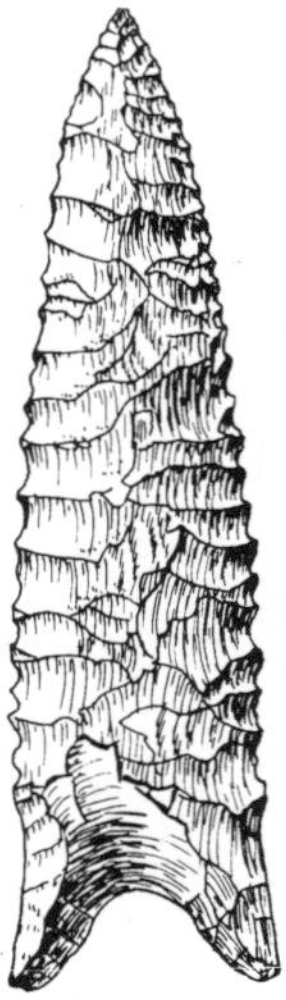

Dalton Serrated

Graham Cave.

The Dalton Serrated forms so characteristic of the Dalton period have wide distribution, almost as broad as that of the Clovis Fluted in the lower Missouri–central Mississippi valley. Dalton Serrated probably is a direct descendant of Clovis Fluted, as the basal thinning of the Dalton Serrated approaches fluting, and they are found with fluted points in the lowest levels at Graham Cave and Rodgers Shelter. In any instance, Dalton Serrated can be used as a diagnostic form of the Dalton period just as successfully as Clovis Fluted has been used for the Paleo-Indian period.

Excavation in Front of Rodgers Shelter

Suggested Reading

Biggs, Robert W., James Stoutamire, and Rain Vehik, 1970. "The Walter Site—A Fluted Point Manifestation in Central Missouri." *Memoir of the Missouri Archaeological Society*, no. 8: 11–60.

Dort, Wakefield, Jr., and J. Knox Jones, Jr., eds., 1970. *Pleistocene and Recent Environments of the Central Great Plains.* The University of Kansas Press, Lawrence.

Goodyear, Albert C., 1974. *The Brand Site: A Techno-functional Study of a Dalton Site in Northeast Arkansas.* Arkansas Archaeological Survey, Research Series no. 7, Fayetteville.

Klippel, Walter E., 1971. "Graham Cave Revisited: A Re-evaluation of Its Cultural Position during the Archaic Period." *Memoir of the Missouri Archaeological Society*, no. 9 (whole volume).

Logan, Wilfred D., 1952. "Graham Cave." *Memoir of the Missouri Archaeological Society*, no. 2: 6–86.

Morse, Dan F., Jr., 1973. "Dalton Culture in Northeast Arkansas." *The Florida Archaeologist* 26(1): 23–38.

Price, James E., and James J. Krakker, 1975. *Dalton Occupation of the Ozark Border.* Museum Briefs no. 20, Museum of Anthropology, University of Missouri, Columbia.

Shippee, J. M., 1964. "Archaeological Remains in the Area of Kansas City: Paleo-Indians and the Archaic Period." *Missouri Archaeological Society Research Series*, no. 2 (whole volume).

Wood, W. Raymond, and R. Bruce McMillan, eds., 1976. *Prehistoric Man and His Environments: A Case Study in the Ozark Highlands.* Academic Press, New York.

The Foragers: Hunter Gatherers of the Archaic Period

The Dalton period is seen as a time of transition from big-game hunting to foraging, to more diversified ways of gaining a living. By the end of the period there was emphasis on the hunting and trapping of small animals and the gathering of wild food plants. The people began to settle in localities where food was more abundant and to adjust their appetites and life-styles to fit the things available to them in their surroundings. The Forager tradition was ushered in by the broadening of subsistence activities and the development of new devices for exploiting new realms. Collecting and hunting on land continued as a major economic practice, but some of the Hunter Gatherers began to collect shellfish or to spend part of the time fishing. Vegetable foods were an important part of their diet. The wandering ways common to the Early Hunters and Hunter Foragers became greatly modified. Foragers began to use a semipermanent camp as a base of operations, to which they returned from their hunting and gathering excursions. These more permanent campsites and the exploitation of a diversity of food resources allowed for an increase in population, but this was gradual and is not apparent in the remains left by those living in the early part of the Archaic period.

The Archaic period, 7000–1000 B.C., has been divided for convenience into Early, Middle, and Late, but it must be remembered that these are time divisions based only in part on cultural changes that took place. Some Foragers changed more rapidly than others; some emphasized shellfishing, some continued to live primarily by hunting, and others gained their subsistence mainly from vegetable products. The artifacts they produced reflected their lifeways only to the extent that they were durable enough for the archaeologist to discover, and usually these were the ones made of stone. Therefore, until very recently when methods have been devised to obtain information on charred vegetable remains from the soil by flotation and other means, we have been dependent primarily on the larger stone and bone tools to interpret what occurred during this early time.

Spear points and knives similar to those of the Hunter Foragers were still being made, but different forms became popular when early Foragers began to experiment with manufacturing techniques. The lanceolate shapes of Early Hunter and Hunter Forager times continued, and basal thinning, reminiscent of earlier fluting techniques, was a step in the manufacture of some knives and dart points. A variety of new forms of stone tools characterize the Forager flint-knapping industry.

Several different forms of cutting tools or spear points appear to be the most popular tool shapes of the first two thousand years of the Archaic period, 7000–5000 B.C. One of these is *Hidden Valley Stemmed*. It was named for Hidden Valley Shelter, located south of the Missouri River on the west bank of the Mississippi, at the eastern edge of Missouri. It was found with other evidences at the bottom level of the shelter, indicating that a group of hunting-gathering people were the first to live there, if only temporarily. Some of their fire hearths were found on the original floor along with knives, spear points, chipped-stone axes, scrapers, and choppers. There were a few of the distinctive Hidden Valley Stemmed and another type characteristic of the Early Archaic period, *Rice Lobed*, named from its occurrence in the lowest levels of Rice Shelter in southwestern Missouri. *Rice Lanceolate* was another Early Archaic form from Rice Shelter.

In northeast Missouri, the Hannibal Complex includes two other cutting tool or projectile point types, *Hardin Barbed* and *St. Charles Notched*. Both were manufactured by Foragers in the early part of the Archaic period.

At Graham Cave the Early Archaic occupation produced a side-notched tool, *Graham Cave Notched*. It demonstrates a new form of preparation of the base for hafting that became very popular during the Middle Archaic. Graham Cave Notched was of widespread occurrence, for it has been found at Rodgers Shelter and on many sites throughout the state.

The lanceolate shape continued in use in the Middle Archaic period, 5000–3000 where it has been called *Agate Basin Lanceolate*. Side notching continued to be a popular form, but it was reduced in size and was less well made. It has been given the name *Big Sandy Notched*. A form that appears to

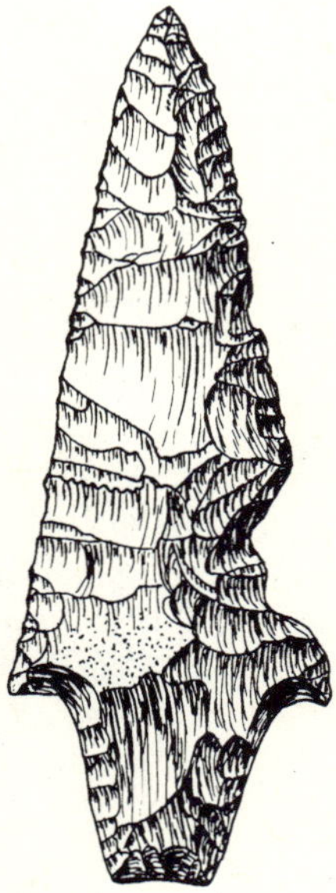

Hidden Valley Stemmed

Graham Cave Notched

Rice Lobed

be limited in distribution to southwestern Missouri was found in Jakie Shelter and has been designated *Jakie Stemmed*. It also occurred in the deposits in Rodgers Shelter.

Toward the beginning of the Middle Archaic two entirely different tool types were developed: the ground stone celt and full-grooved ax. The full-grooved ax was made by the Foragers in Jakie Shelter and in Graham Cave and is a characteristic tool of the Middle Archaic period. Twined-bag impressions in moist clay that subsequently hardened in drying were preserved in Graham Cave. They are proof of a finger-weaving industry that probably was as early, or earlier, than the Early Archaic and continued until the cave was abandoned in the Late Woodland period. The knowledge of making tools by pecking and grinding presumably began in the Dalton period, where mortars and pestles are present, but the stone-working technology did not become a major activity until the Late Archaic period. The fact that the prevalence of the pecked-and-ground stone ax is used as a time marker for the Middle Archaic, a means of separating it from the Early Archaic, does not mean that the form appeared suddenly or was restricted to that one period. There are developmental predecessors of all forms that later become time and cultural markers, and the forms often appear in two or more periods and cultural complexes.

The Indians who used the shelters and caves in Missouri were living in the state fairly continuously, but utilized the rock shelters and caves only

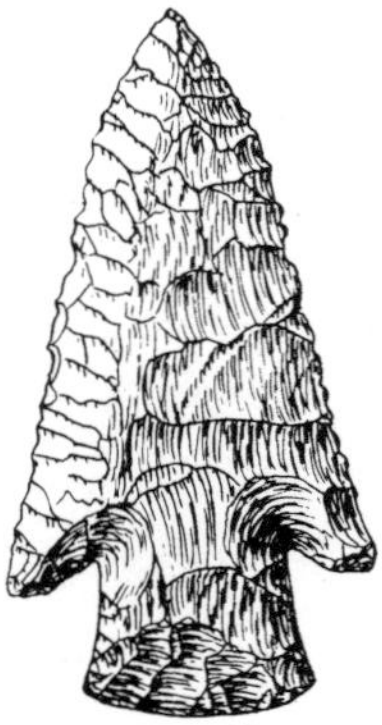

Hardin Barbed

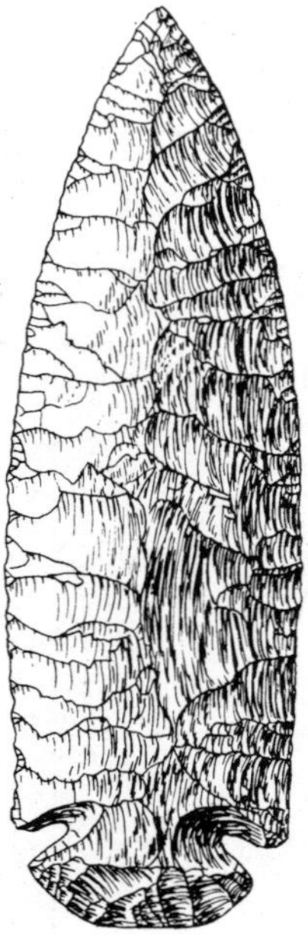

St. Charles Notched

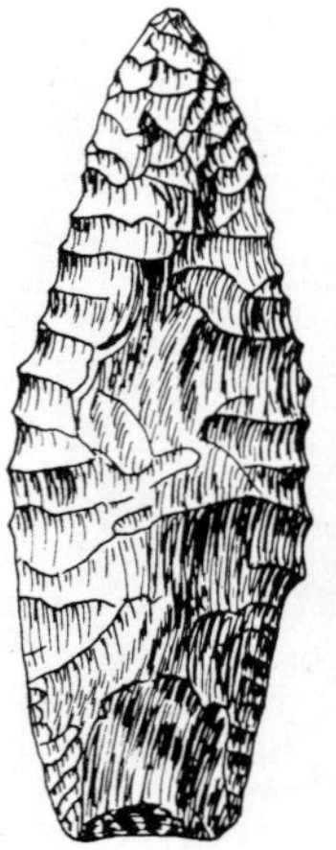

Rice Lanceolate

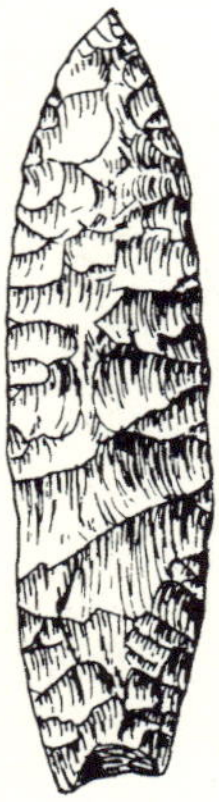

Agate Basin
Lanceolate

Big Sandy
Notched

Jakie Stemmed

Fabric Impression

occasionally as stops for short periods while on hunting or gathering trips. Although there was a gradual development in the use of various tools and implements, the changes seem to appear quickly and dramatically when the deposits represent occasional long periods of abandonment. Furthermore, there is never a full complement of the tools or activities of the people represented by the deposits in any single site. Since much of the sequence of cultural development in Missouri has been obtained from caves and shelters, the separation of the Archaic into Early, Middle, and Late periods is somewhat arbitrary and subject to change as more information becomes available.

There is little question that the Foragers in the Late Archaic period, 3000–1000 B.C., made dart points that were different from those in preceding periods. One of them, a small point with a base ground smooth, was first identified in the Table Rock Reservoir area and has been named *Table Rock Stemmed*. Another, quite different in shape and manufacture, is called

4.2

Groundstone Celt,
Jakie Shelter

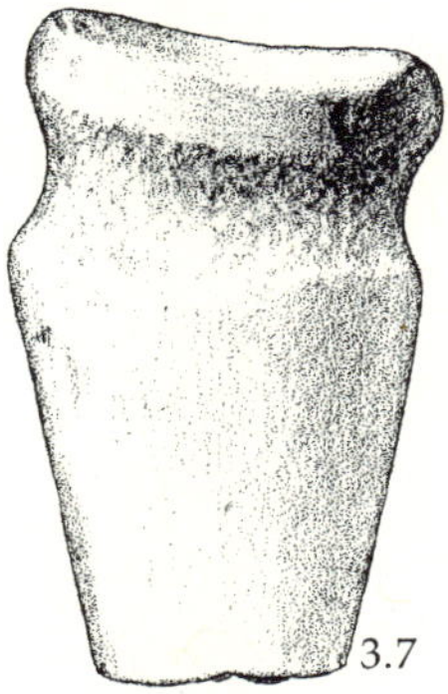

3.7

Full-Grooved Ax,
Jakie Shelter

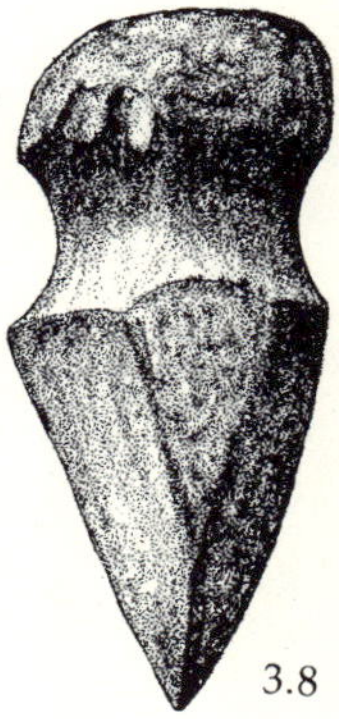

3.8

Full-Grooved Ax,
Graham Cave

Afton Corner Notched, for it was first found in large quantity in a spring near Afton, Oklahoma.

The south-central part of Missouri was the center of the homeland of another group of Late Archaic period Foragers named the Sedalia phase because their campsites clustered around the modern city of Sedalia. The Sedalia phase people made a very distinctive spearpoint or knife, lanceolate in shape, that has been named *Sedalia Lanceolate*. Another distinctive item manufactured by these foragers is an adz or scraper called the *Clear Fork Gouge* from a site in Texas. It is triangular, made from a large spall of flint, unworked on one side and snubbed off on the broad end to form a cutting edge similar to that of an adz. Use polish on one surface, and sometimes both, indicates that it was employed as an adz, or scraper. Another tool occurring almost as frequently is rectanguloid or ovoid and bifacially flaked. Since it usually has polish on both sides from having been a digging tool, it is named *Sedalia Digger*. Such artifacts are numerous on the surface of sites in the Sedalia area and were very important to the people that produced them. Large basal-notched (called *Smith Basal Notched*) and stemmed (named *Etley Stemmed*) spear points or knives, and drills formed by reworking those types and Sedalia Lanceolate, are other artifacts from Sedalia phase sites.

The people lived in relatively small villages high on the hills overlooking streams that were often quite far from the major streams. One camp

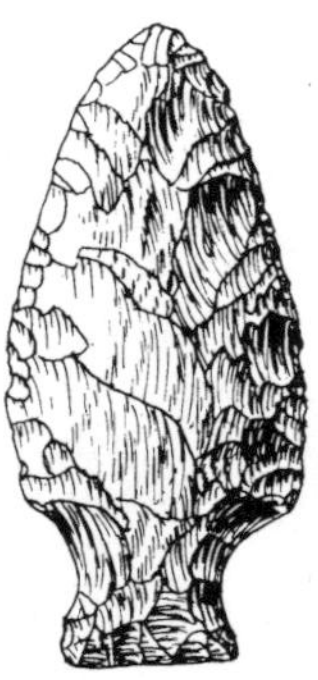

Table Rock Stemmed

Afton Corner Notched

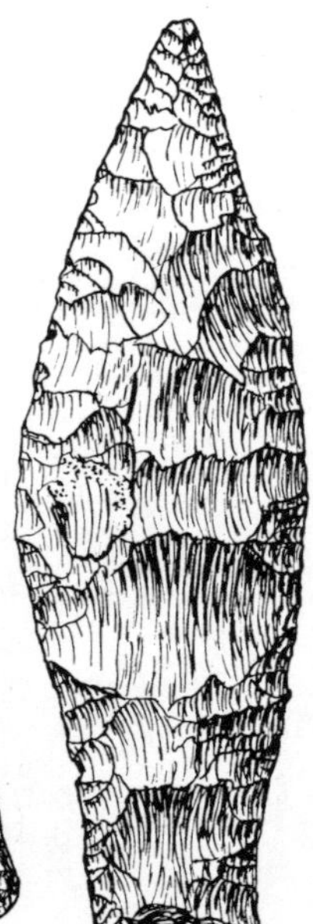

Sedalia Lanceolate

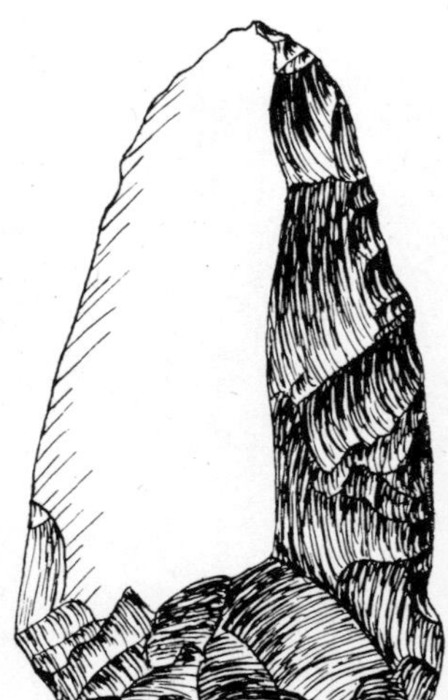

Clear Fork Gouge

location, the Geiger site, has six circular dark-colored soil areas lined up along the south slope of a hill near the Missouri River. These may have been the location of house sites, but evidence to confirm the interpretation has not been forthcoming.

The Sedalia phase is closely related to the *Nebo Hill phase,* near Kansas City, which is thought to have developed earlier but continued throughout the Late Archaic period. The *Nebo Hill Lanceolate* is quite distinctive but is similar enough to the Sedalia Lanceolate that it may have been its progenitor. Other distinctive Nebo Hill items are pecked-and-ground stone celts, three-quarter-grooved axes, and shaped manos.

A secondary center of the Sedalia phase has been identified in the northeast prairie region of Missouri. It is represented by the Booth site on Salt River in the Cannon Reservoir area. *Stone Square-Stemmed* was one of the large knife or projectile point forms in the assemblage, along with manos and metates, not previously mentioned as artifacts associated with the Sedalia phase. The manos and metates denote that the Booth site was a base of operations for collecting and processing plant foods. There was no

Sedalia Digger 6.6

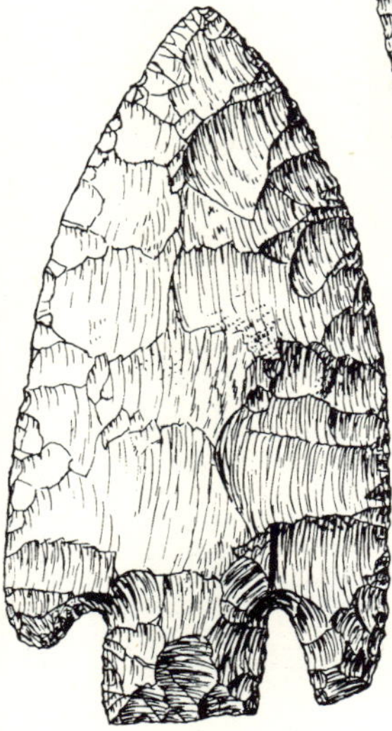

Smith Basal Notched

Drill

Etley Stemmed

evidence that hunting was an important activity. This emphasis on gathering rather than hunting appears to be a characteristic of all Sedalia phase sites.

In the Late Archaic period the Hunter-Gatherers evidently believed strongly in an afterlife, and ceremonies associated with the dead were elaborate. The dead were frequently buried with accompanying goods. Partial burial, which is burial of parts of the body or of an incomplete body, was characteristic.

In the central part of the northeast region of Missouri, near Troy in Lincoln County, evidences found on a burial site overlooking Cuivre River have been called the Cuivre River Ceremonial Complex, a component of the Sedalia phase. The site has been excavated fully enough to give some insight into the funeral practices and beliefs as well as knowledge about the implements the Cuivre people considered important enough to place with their dead. The method used in the burial of their dead indicates that the people devoted much attention to the dead and expressed a definite belief in an afterlife. These were made in a cemetery area, and secondary burials, or deposits of bundles of bones rather than of the body in the flesh, were customary. Each bundle of bones had with it lanceolate-shaped knives (*Red Ochre Lanceolate*), spearheads, or grooved axes. Bodies of the dead may have been exposed in trees or on platforms until nothing but the bones remained and then bundled and buried, no doubt with some ceremony, in the cemetery. Placed with the bones of the individual were the

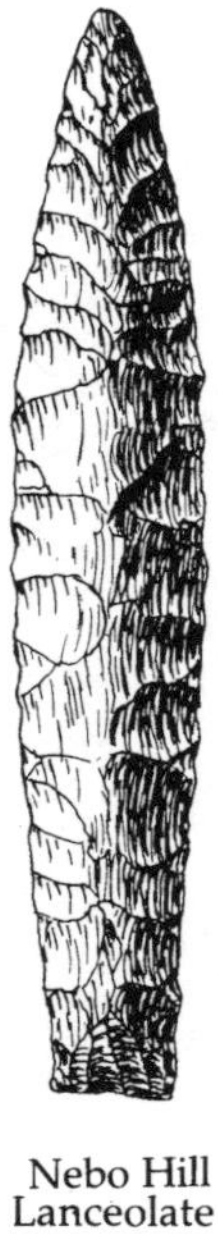

Nebo Hill Lanceolate

Stone Square Stemmed

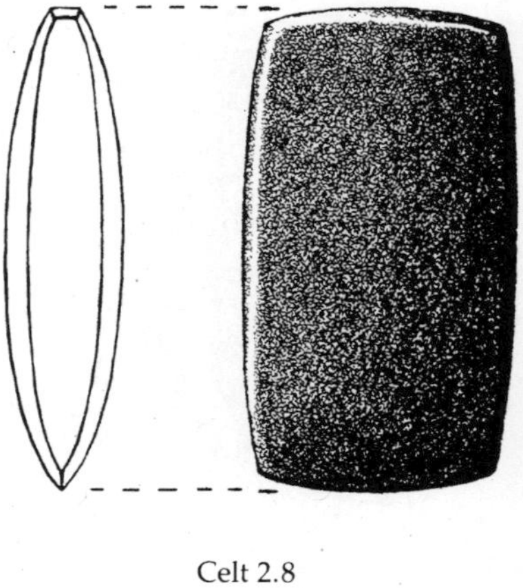

Celt 2.8

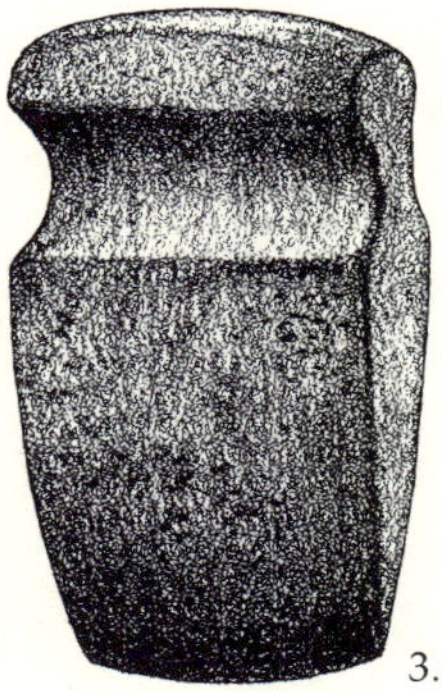

3.8

Three-Quarter-Grooved Ax

5.3

Shaped Mano

special tools, indicating belief that they would be needed in afterlife. The fact that the Cuivre River people buried their dead in cemeteries also points to the probability that the burial ceremony was a function of the group rather than of the individual. Such group action in connection with the disposal of the dead can be considered religious in nature.

Another component of the Cuivre River Ceremonial Complex is the Hatton Mound, where a great variety of items were found. Burials were flexed or bundled, or were piles or scatters of bone. Caches of offerings had been placed with the bones in a large, shallow, oval depression also containing chert cobbles and boulders. Two large cutting tools were Etleylike and Sedalialike, but must be considered as specially made rather than typical.

In the western edge of Illinois, and perhaps extending across the Mississippi River into Missouri, is an aggregate derived from several sites that has been given the name *Titterington focus.* Included among the typical artifacts of the aggregate is a variety of items that may also be characteristic of the Late Archaic period. Spear-thrower weights or bannerstones were added to spear throwers, perhaps as much for luck and magic as for increased efficiency. A bannerstone added charm as well as impetus to the flight of the dart from the spear thrower. Stone gorgets were worn at the throat, and other polished and perforated ornaments decorated the arms and chest.

The Archaic period was one of experimentation, borrowing, and amalgamation of ideas and techniques for obtaining a living and for developing tools as aids in such endeavors. Other ground-stone objects of distinctive shape made by the Foragers included plummets or bola weights. The ground-stone ungrooved ax was frequent. Full-grooved axes, characteristic tools in the Middle Archaic, continued to be used and a new form, the three-quarter-grooved ax, took precedence over the full grooved in the Late Archaic.

The typical spear and cutting tool shapes changed to side notched, basal notched, and stemmed forms. Dart points were hafted in foreshafts that were in turn inserted in the long spear shafts rather than directly on the end.

Finger weaving, a twined weaving technique using plant fibers, was practiced during the Archaic period; the making of thread and cordage from sinew, hair, and fiber was an old trait probably stemming from the earliest appearance of mankind on the North American continent. Bone was used more prominently in the later periods, as was wood, and consequently a carving tool, the adz, became a characteristic implement of some

Red Ochre Lanceolate

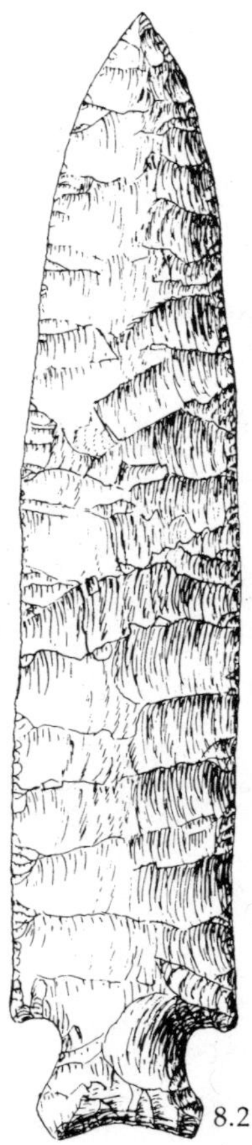

8.2

Etleylike Stemmed

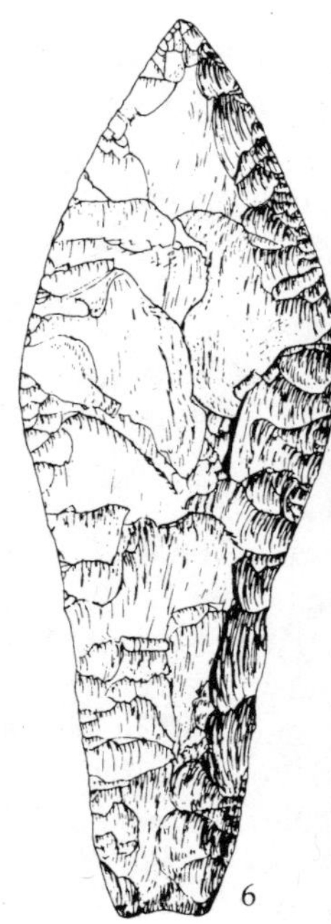

6

Sedalialike Lanceolate

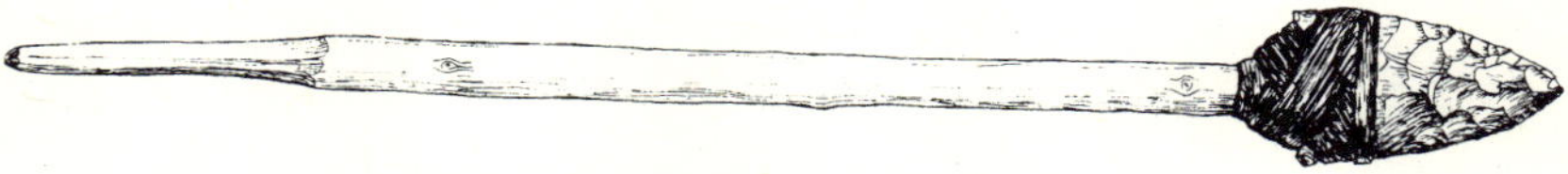

Foreshaft and Hafted Dart Point

5.3

Wooden Foreshaft

of the Foragers, particularly those in west-central and northeastern Missouri.

The Forager culture through the Early, Middle, and Late Archaic periods was one of change and adaptation to the climatic, physiographic, faunal, and floral environments. The Archaic lasted throughout a period estimated to be six thousand years long, during which cultural developments taking place in the north, east, south, and west were transferred to the Foragers in the lower Missouri–central Mississippi valley.

Gorget

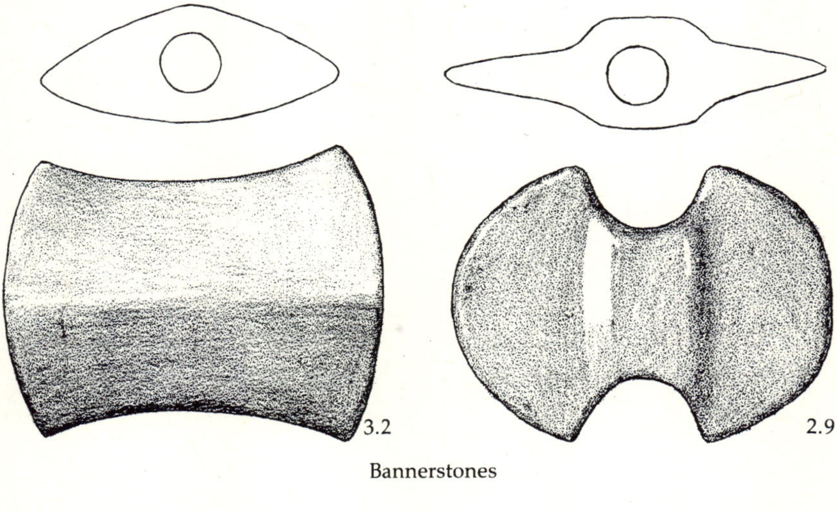

3.2 2.9

Bannerstones

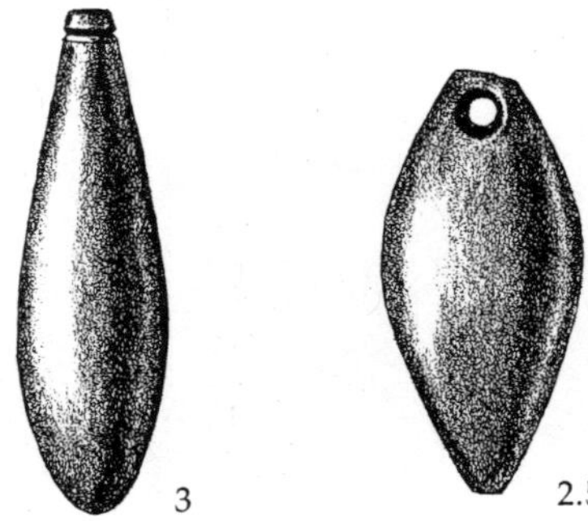

3 2.5 Plummets

Suggested Reading

American Antiquity, 1959. Five papers on the Archaic. 24(3):229–318.

Bacon, W. S., and W. J. Miller, 1957. "Notes on the Excavation of a Burial Area in Northeast Missouri." *The Missouri Archaeologist* 19(3): 19–34.

Cook, Thomas Genn, 1976. *Koster: An Artifact Analysis of Two Archaic Phases in West-Central Illinois*. Northwestern University Archaeological Program, Evanston, Illinois.

Johnson, Alfred E., ed., 1980. *Archaic Prehistory on the Prairie-Plains Border*. University of Kansas Publications in Anthropology, no. 12, Lawrence.

Klippel, Walter E., 1969. *The Booth Site: A Late Archaic Campsite*. Missouri Archaeological Society Research Series, no. 6.

Lewis, Thomas N., and Madeline Kneberg Lewis, 1961. *Eva, an Archaic Site*. University of Tennessee Press, Knoxville.

Shippee, J. M., 1966. "The Archaeology of Arnold Research Cave, Callaway County, Missouri." *The Missouri Archaeologist* 28: 1–40.

Struever, Stuart, and Felicia Antonelli Holton, 1979. *Koster Americans in Search of Their Prehistoric Past*. Anchor Press/Doubleday, Garden City, New York.

The First Potters: Early Woodland Period

In the central and southeastern parts of Missouri and in the whole lower Mississippi River Valley a new development, the firing of clay tools and utensils, was beginning to gain momentum. The old way of life, which utilized stone, bone, wood, and shell for tools and utensils, was taking a major step forward. The customs of hunting with the spear thrower and spears, the use of spear-thrower weights, and the use of gorgets remained as symbols of the habits of old. Clay balls, perhaps used as sling balls or bola balls, became prevalent. The molding and firing of clay balls and other items was an innovation that was becoming widespread and popular, and, most progressive of all, pottery vessels came into use. The introduction of pottery brought the Archaic period to a close.

Again it is obvious that the invention of pottery was not a spur of the moment discovery occurring at a definite time, but a gradual development which took place over a fairly long period and which probably changed under influences deriving from different areas and directions.

The acquisition of the knowledge of potterymaking by the Foragers was a significant step toward their settlement in one place for a long time. The women manufactured durable containers which made possible the storage of seeds, the stewing of food, and the transportation and storage of water. Most important to the archaeologist, pottery provides a time indicator as well as an evidence of cultural change, both reflected in decorative styles, vessel shapes, and methods of pottery manufacture.

The early part of the Woodland period, the period of the first potters, is little known. The period began perhaps as early as 1000 B.C. and lasted until about 500 B.C. Pottery was enough of a novelty that it was transported on hunting trips, and parts of the vessels so transported and accidentally broken are found in cave sites used as temporary shelter by hunting parties of the early potters. The spear and spear thrower was still the primary weapon.

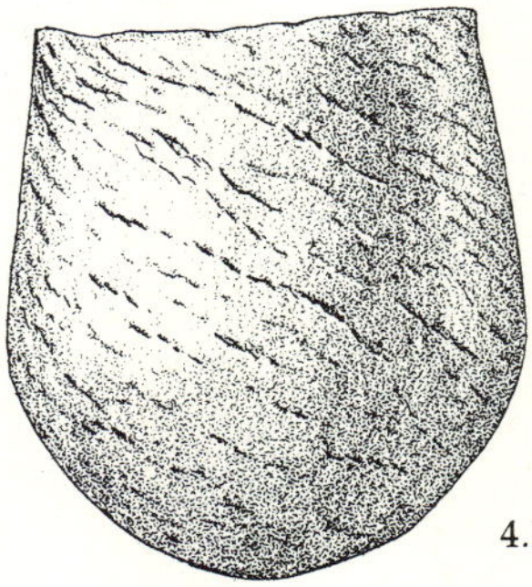

4.2

Liverpool Cord Marked

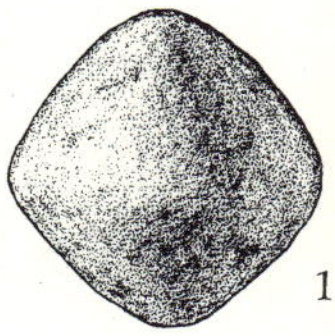

1.8

Clay Ball

In the lower Missouri Valley, the change may have come from the north. The earliest pottery, Black Sand Incised, is an addition to the Archaic stonework on small campsites. The pottery is sand-tempered and decorated with incised lines, the incised decoration often being cut on top of cord marking. *Black Sand Incised* was first found in Illinois. The manufacturers of the Black Sand type of vessels left bits of their distinctive pottery sherds from central Missouri to central Illinois. Another type of Early Woodland pottery decorated with cord impressions has been named *Liverpool Cord Marked*.

In southeastern Missouri the early pottery makers manufactured and decorated a clay-tempered pottery that was added to the preceding Late Archaic culture in that area. At the Burkett site in Mississippi County, the change to the use of pottery demonstrates the cultural change from the Archaic to the Woodland. The typical dart point made by the Burkett people, *Burkett stemmed,* was rather large and thick and was contracting stemmed.

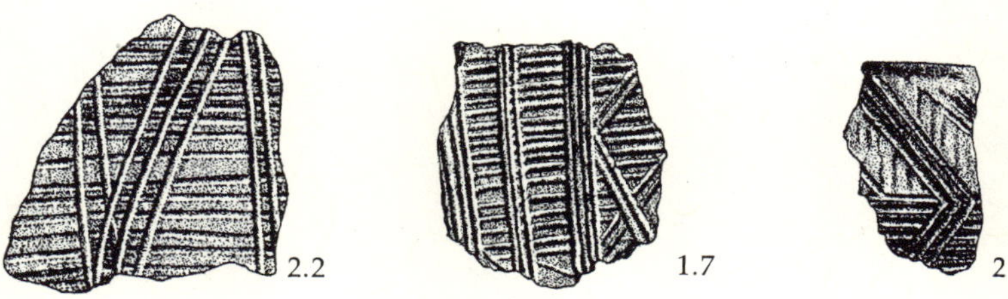

Black Sand Pottery Sherds

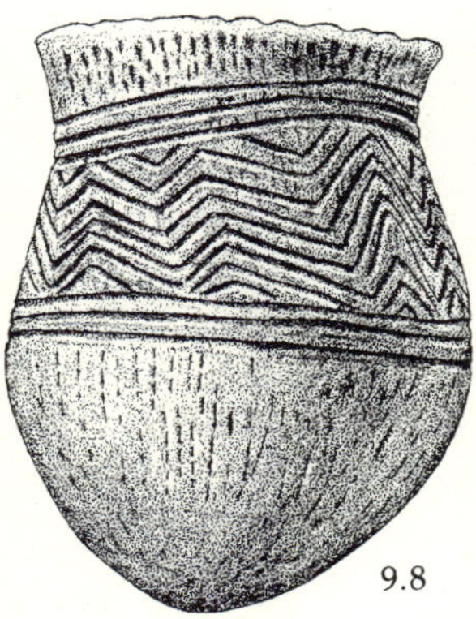

Black Sand Incised

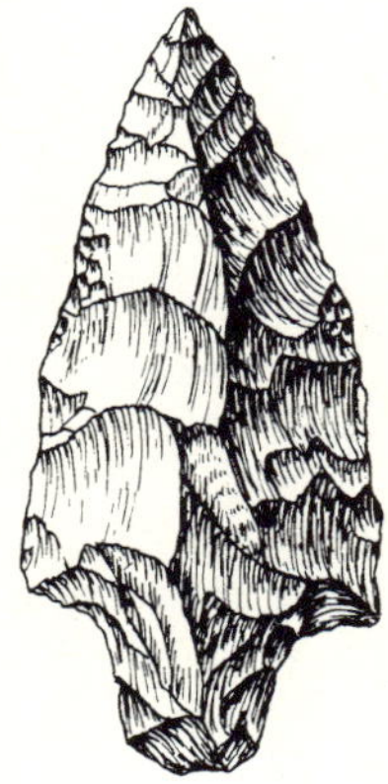

Burkett Stemmed

Suggested Reading

Dragoo, Don W., 1976. "Some Aspects of Eastern North American Prehistory: A Review, 1975." *American Antiquity* 41(1): 3–27.

Griffin, James B., 1967. "Eastern North American Archaeology: A Summary." *Science* 156(3772): 175–91.

The Traders: Middle Woodland Period

Gardening, the settlement in one place for a long period of time by well-organized communities, the construction of large ceremonial earthworks, widespread trading, and the manufacture of a great variety of excellently made art objects distinguished the Middle Woodland period people from their predecessors. The growing of corn and locally domesticated plants was an added economic activity but was not as important as hunting and gathering. It was probably the development of a more efficient control over hunting and gathering and the organization of large numbers of people for certain tasks rather than the increase in the food supply by gardening that made it possible for the people of the community to allot the time necessary to build the mounds, ditches, and embankments associated with their ceremonial life. Trade was very important to their economy, as the emphasis upon ceremony and ritual objects accounted for the widespread trading and exchange to the east, the south, the far west, and the north for special materials to be made into art objects. Hides, furs, and foodstuffs must have been exchanged along with the exotic materials. Cultural development during this Middle Woodland period, 500 B.C.–A.D. 400, was strong and vigorous and spread over most of the Midwest.

The new, expanded cultural activity in the Mississippi River drainage area had a major center in Ohio and adjacent states bordering the Ohio River. The culture there has been named *Hopewell,* the name of the landowner upon whose farm Middle Woodland period earthworks were excavated and described by early archaeologists. This name has been used also to designate the whole spread of the culture throughout the Missouri-Mississippi River Valley. It is also called the *Hopewellian Interaction Sphere.* There were centers in Illinois, Missouri, Oklahoma, Arkansas, Louisiana, and Mississippi, and related developments extended to New York, Pennsylvania, Michigan, Wisconsin, Minnesota, and Iowa.

The Hopewell who lived in Ohio reached great heights in the development of the arts and in the construction of elaborate earthworks. They possessed a great variety of items that denote the extent of their trade—mica from the Appalachian Mountains, conch shells from the Gulf of

8

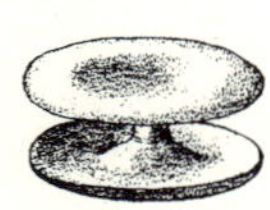
2

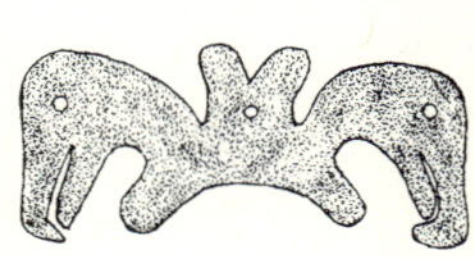
4.7

Copper Earspool and Ornaments

Mexico, obsidian from the Rocky Mountains, and native copper from the Great Lakes. The Hopewell were the first Indians in the midwestern region to maintain settlements in one place for long periods and to devote some of their time to growing corn, but it was too limited in quantity to be a staple crop. It probably was considered a sacred plant and was grown for use in ceremonies. Game was most important to the diet and must have been obtained by communal hunts. Well-organized fishing and the gathering of nuts, seeds, and berries when they ripened were major supplements to the diet. Pottery vessels were manufactured in large quantities and were greatly elaborated in shape and decoration. A characteristic vessel is called *Hopewell Zoned Incised*. Both jar and bowl shapes were common, and the bases of the vessels varied from round to flat and occasionally had four feet. The rim, shoulder, and body of the vessels were decorated by the techniques of incising, punctating, and stamping. On the bodies of some vessels, areas filled with dentate stamping were separated by undecorated areas to make up an overall pattern of design.

Eastern Hopewell

6.5

Hopewell Zoned Incised

3.6

Wolf Effigy Stone Pipe

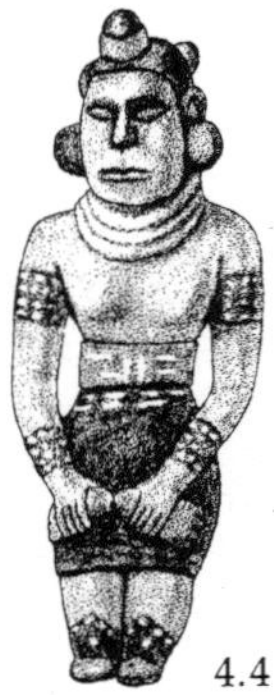

4.4

Figurine

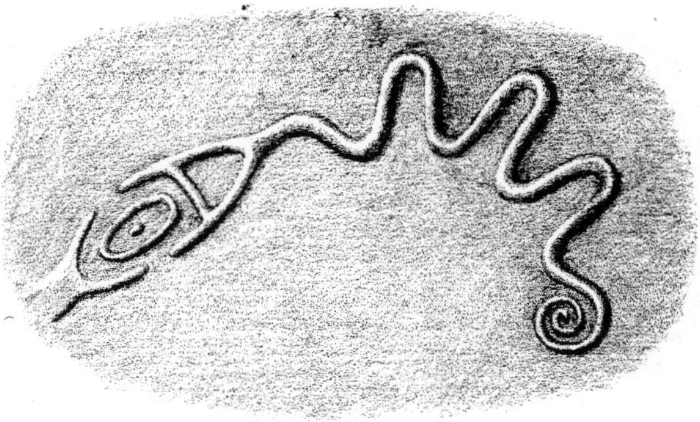

Great Serpent Mound

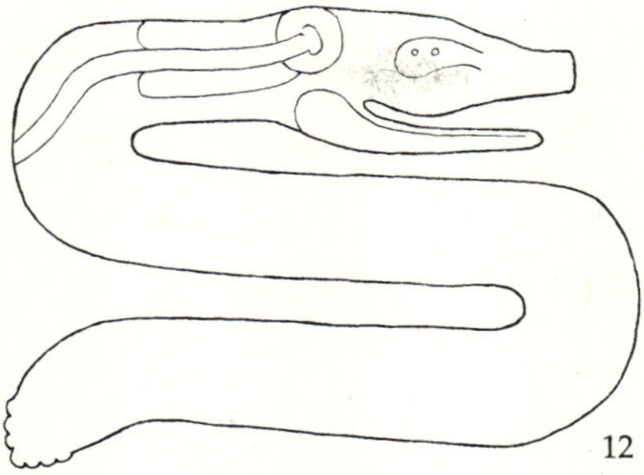

12

Mica Ornament

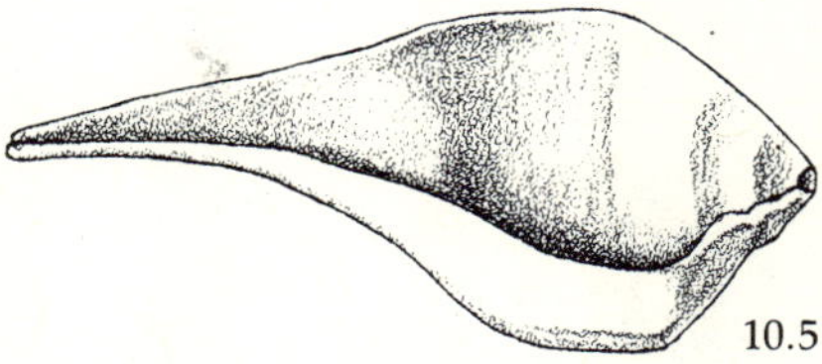

10.5

Shell Dipper

People from the Hopewell villages often assembled in special localities to conduct ceremonies. At these sacred places were geometric earthworks consisting of ditches and embankments enclosing burial mounds, or earthworks constructed in the shape of animals, such as the Great Serpent Mound in Ohio. Some of the earthworks were built on hilltops, and their location in defensible positions has led to their being called forts. Perhaps they were, but they may just as well have been for the more peaceful purpose of providing a secluded place for conducting dances and ceremonies in honor of the dead.

Outstanding examples of Hopewell art are the sculptured stone pipes, many of which depict men and animals. Small clay figurines are finely modeled and are painted to show details of clothing. Hammered copper ornaments of pleasing design were probably used on ceremonial dress, and designs cut out of large sheets of mica may also have adorned clothing for special purposes. Ingenious spool-shaped ornaments hammered from

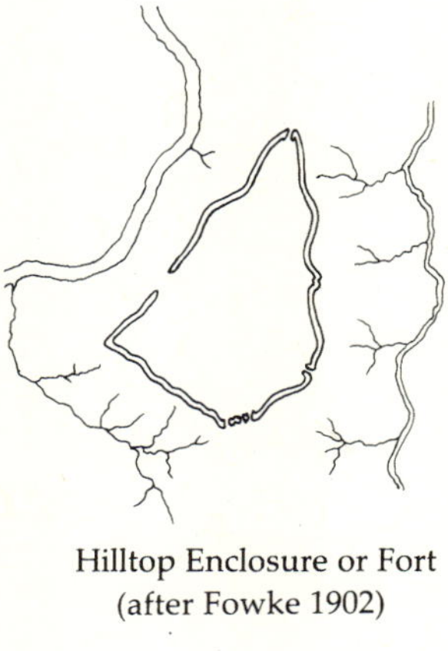

Hilltop Enclosure or Fort
(after Fowke 1902)

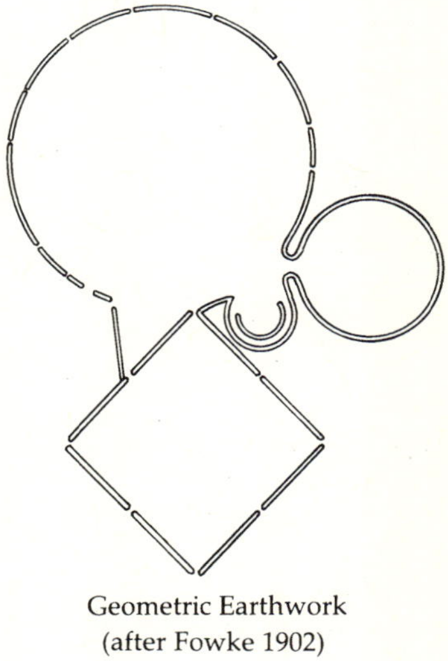

Geometric Earthwork
(after Fowke 1902)

9

Obsidian Ceremonial Knife

thin sheets of copper were attached to the earlobes. Large flaked obsidian knives and conch or whelk shell dippers made up part of the paraphernalia associated with ceremony. All of these items were skillfully manufactured, and many of them are outstanding examples of pre-Columbian art.

It has been assumed that the Hopewell people living east of the Mississippi River migrated west to Missouri because the Hopewell of the Middle Woodland period in the state appeared suddenly about the beginning of the Christian Era of the Old World. There was a general concentration of Hopewell settlements frm the mouth of the Lamine River to the mouth of the Kansas River along the Missouri River. The people were pioneers, and in their move to the West they came in contact with roving tribes and adopted some of their ways of life. As with all pioneers, they had left many of the benefits of a more settled life behind. Their villages in Missouri were smaller than those they had left, and so were their gardens. Hunting was more important in the getting of food, and this left less time and fewer people to build the large ceremonial earthworks. Trade, though widespread, was not a paramount activity and probably was secondary to the long hunting trips in search of game. In effect, the full force of Hopewell culture may not have reached the central parts of Missouri.

The Hopewell people who lived in Missouri, though closely related to the Hopewellian Interaction Sphere in Illinois and elsewhere, had their distinctive cultural features. Like all those involved in the Hopewellian trading interaction, hunting game and gathering wild fruits, berries, and nuts were part of their subsistence activities. Fishing also supplied a portion of their diet, and corn was grown in their gardens. Unlike the Hopewell in Ohio, little time was spent on building ceremonial earthworks, and mounds for the dead were comparatively small. A great deal more time was spent on means of acquiring food than on ceremony.

Deer and wild turkey were the main game animals and furnished not only food but also bones for tools and skins and feathers for clothing. Stone dart points (*Steuben Expanded Stemmed*) were manufactured in large quantities as well as stone flake knives (blades) and scrapers for use in the process of making clothing of animal skins, furs, and feathers. Heat treating of the flint was a step in the manufacturing process of chipped stone tools. Cores, when reduced to a size too small to produce blades long enough to be used as cutting tools, were discarded or were converted into scrapers.

The production of large numbers of pottery vessels may have been in connection with increased gardening and gathering. Gathered nuts,

1.9

Scraper

1.7

Blade

Core (side view)
natural size

Steuben Expanded
Stemmed

fruits, seeds, and corn from the garden had to be dehydrated before they could be stored successfully for long periods. In turn, before eating them, the dried foods were soaked and cooked in the watertight fired clay vessels. Pottery was of two main shapes, jars and bowls. The jars, especially the larger ones, were cooking vessels and usually were not as highly decorated as the bowls and the smaller vessels which may have been used for ceremonial purposes and for personal use. Decorations are much the same as those found on the pottery vessels in the Ohio region and characteristically consist of crosshatching on the rim and punctations, rocker marking, dentate stamping, and zoned areas set apart by incising along the rim, shoulder, and body. The pattern of the design on the body of the vessel sometimes is elaborate, although in most instances designs are in simple units that extend horizontally around the vessel between the rim and the shoulder or between the rim and the base. The pottery was tempered with crushed grit and was manufactured by the coiling method.

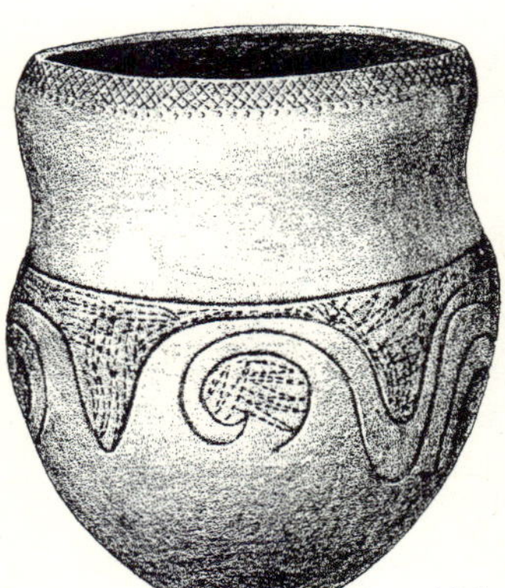

11.5

Pottery Jar

3

Pottery Bowl

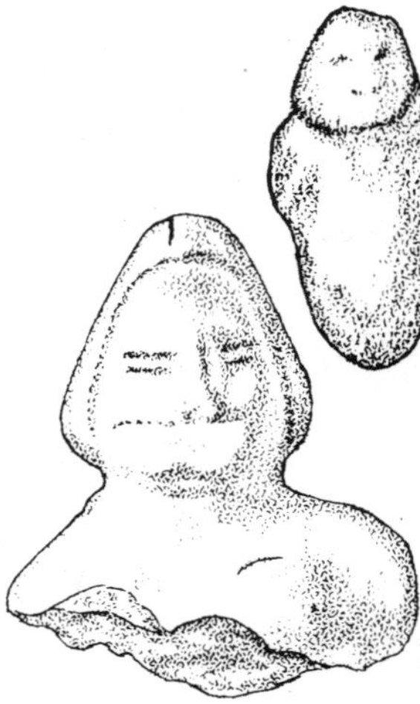

1.4 1.9 1.7

Figurines and Figurine Head

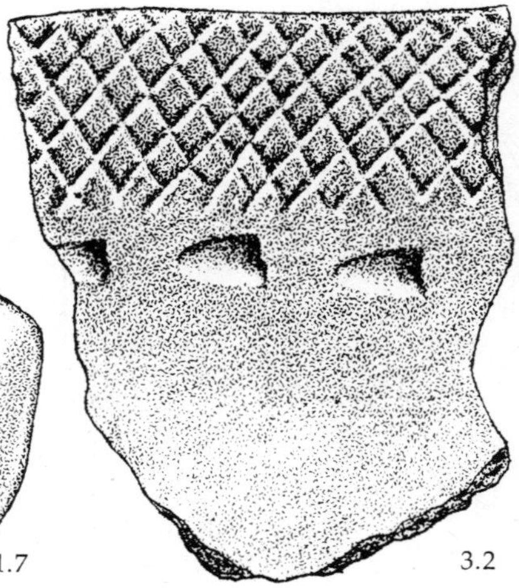

3.2

Renner Crosshatched Rim

It is a distinctive Hopewell item, very easily recognized. In Missouri *Renner Crosshatched Rim* is a typical decoration.

In most instances, artifacts were made of stone, bone, pottery, and shell, and the manufacture of items from trade goods was not very extensive. A few celts, adzes, awls, and beads were made from native copper. Mica was sometimes used in sheets, but was not shaped into decorative ornaments. Conch shells were not unknown, but they were cut to form beads, not used whole. Evidently the artisans who fabricated the ceremonial pipes and ornaments in the Ohio area seldom traveled west to Missouri, and few

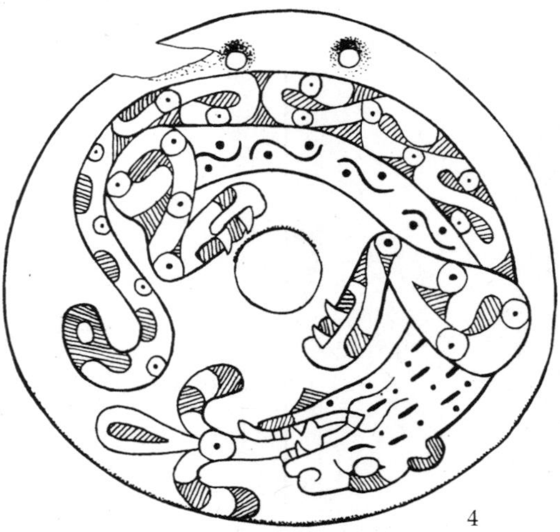

4

Engraved Shell Gorget (Jaguar)

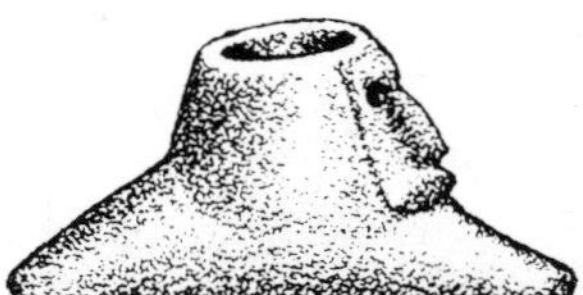

3

Sculptured Stone Pipe

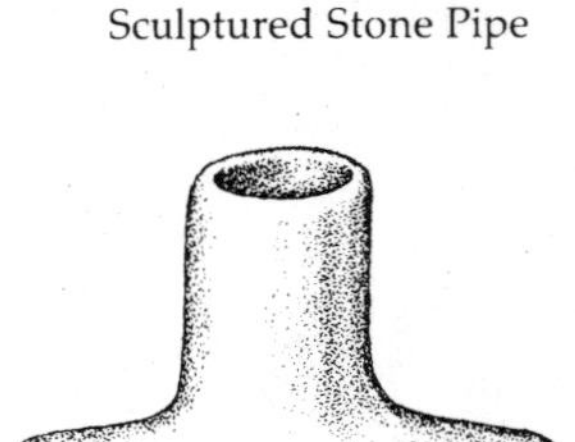

2.3

Clay Pipe

of their products filtered into the area through exchange. One conch shell pendant from southwest Missouri, found in a rock cairn lying between the Hopewellian centers in Missouri and that in northeast Oklahoma, has been identified as Hopewell, but it could just as easily have been made by later people. Since it has a jaguar depicted on its surface, and the northern range of the jaguar is limited to Texas, New Mexico, and Arizona, it would appear to relate to the Southwest, where no Hopewell centers are found. Most of the clay figurines found in central and western Missouri lack the realism and detail of those found in Illinois or Ohio. Pipes are simpler, with few being sculptured. The paraphernalia manufactured from exotic materials such as copper, mica, obsidian, and sea shells was very limited in the centers on the Missouri River. Perhaps this was due to the great distance from the Illinois and Ohio centers resulting in less interaction and exchange with them. Another possible explanation is that the people residing there were pioneers, leaving behind many of the niceties of the developed centers to the east. For whatever reason, a number of the art forms produced in exotic materials, distinctive items in the Hopewell of Illinois and Ohio, were lacking.

The construction of earthworks and mounds for burial of the dead was a very important activity, but it never reached the intense development attained in Ohio. In the central Missouri area in Saline County, the Hopewell people may have built an earthwork called "The Old Fort," which is preserved in Van Meter State Park. This earthwork is made up of a series of ditches and embankments enclosing burial mounds. The whole

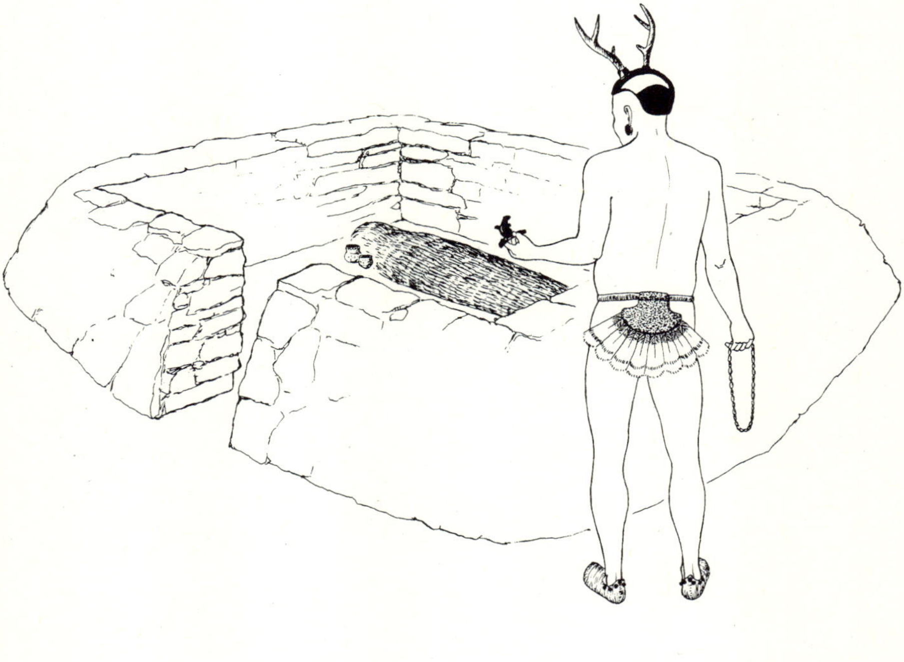

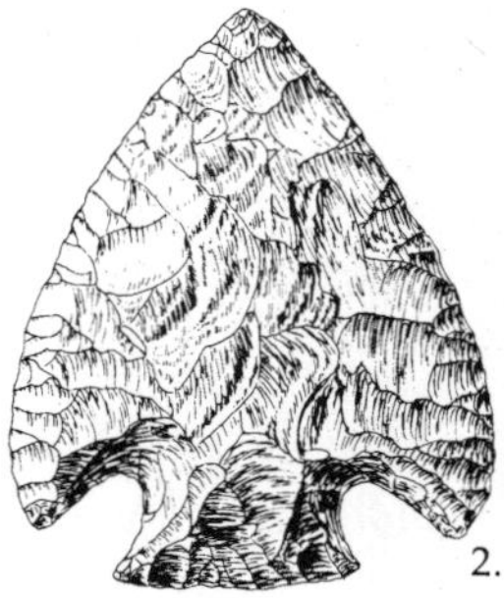

2.7

Snyders Notched

2.9

Frog Effigy Pipe

encompasses an area of 6.2 acres. Less spectacular earthworks covering stone chambers are of a distinctive type. The chambers, square or rectangular in construction, with an entranceway on one side, were receptacles for the dead. The chambers were sometimes roofed with logs and then covered with earth. Burial customs associated with the Hopewell were varied; cremation and the subsequent placement of the ashes and burned bones was practiced as well as burial in the flesh in the stone chambers inside the burial mounds.

The Hopewell people who lived in the west-central part of Missouri were in a process of change. Their way of life furnished the basis for the Late Woodland cultures that followed them. Since the main bases of the Middle and Late Woodland cultures were the same and the change was gradual, it is not always easily possible to separate the two.

1.4

Figurine Head

3.3

Figurine

Reconstructed Figurine

In the northeastern part of Missouri, along the Mississippi River, the Hopewell occupation related so closely to that in Illinois that it can be included with the Illinois Havana center. Pipes were sometimes beautifully sculptured, and clay figurines were much more lifelike. The *Snyders Notched* projectile point or knife typical of the Illinois Hopewell was commonly used.

Suggested Reading

Brose, David S., and N'omi Greber, eds., 1979. *Hopewell Archaeology: The Chillicothe Conference.* Kent State University Press, Kent, Ohio.

Caldwell, Joseph R., and Robert L. Hall, eds., 1964. *Hopewellian Studies.* Illinois State Museum Scientific Papers, vol. 12.

Chapman, Carl H., 1980. *The Archaeology of Missouri, II.* University of Missouri Press, Columbia.

Deuel, Thorne, ed., 1954. *Hopewellian Communities in Illinois.* Illinois State Museum Scientific Papers, vol. 5.

Griffin, James B., 1958. *The Chronological Position of the Hopewellian Culture in the Eastern United States.* Anthropological Papers, Museum of Anthropology, University of Michigan, no. 12.

Johnson, Alfred E., ed., 1976. *Hopewellian Archaeology in the Lower Missouri Valley.* University of Kansas Publications in Anthropology, no. 8, Lawrence.

Johnson, Alfred E., 1981. "Kansas City Hopewell Subsistence and Settlement System." *The Missouri Archaeologist* 42: 69–76.

Kay, Marvin, 1975. "Social Distance among Central Missouri Hopewell Settlements: A First Approximation." *American Antiquity* 40(1): 64–67.

Kay, Marvin, 1980. *Central Missouri Hopewell Subsistence-Settlement System.* Missouri Archaeological Society Research Series, no. 15.

Kay, Marvin, and Alfred E. Johnson, 1977. "Havana Tradition Chronology of Central Missouri." *Midcontinental Journal of Archaeology* 2(2): 195–217.

Roedl, Leo J., and James H. Howard, 1957. "Archaeological Investigations at the Renner Site." *The Missouri Archaeologist* 19(1–2): 53–90.

Struever, Stuart, 1968. "Woodland Subsistence-Settlement Systems in the Lower Illinois Valley." In *New Perspectives in Archaeology*, edited by S. R. Binford and L. R. Binford, pp. 285–312, Aldine Press, Chicago.

Struever, Stuart, and Gail L. Houart, 1972. "An Analysis of the Hopewell Interaction Sphere." *Anthropological Papers, Museum of Anthropology, University of Michigan*, no. 46: 47–79.

Wedel, Waldo R., 1943. *Archaeological Investigations in Platte and Clay Counties, Missouri.* U.S. National Museum Bulletin 183, Government Printing Office, Washington, D.C.

The Regional Isolationists: Late Woodland Period

The religious cult that tightly bound the Hopewell people to expending much of their time and energy on ceremonies honoring the dead began to loosen and to dissipate toward the latter part of the Middle Woodland period. The ceremonial controls evident in the Hopewell had disintegrated. The widespread trading that had occurred earlier in contacts across most of the central United States, from the headwaters of the entire Mississippi drainage to its mouth, no longer was important and may not have been possible. There seems to have been a breakdown of communication and trade between the different regions, and localities were isolated from each other. Local varieties of culture developed, most of which were a regression from the Hopewell that preceded them.

The change, though gradual, was occurring over the entire area of the eastern United States. In the central Ozark Highland area of Missouri there was an unelaborated village life that had not been affected by the Hopewell development. This was understandable in view of the isolation of many villages and the lack of general contact, which was difficult to maintain in an area of deep valleys separated by narrow ridges and expanses of prairie. The strongest developments of the regionally isolated cultures that had broken down from the Hopewell came at the edges of the areas least populated by the Middle Woodland people in the preceding period. For example, upon the disappearance of the Hopewell, the isolated bands that were living in the northeastern area and in the Ozark Highland, which had only occasional contact with the Hopewell traders, seemingly expanded into numerous villages. These small bands of potters, adapted to both the prairie and forest, moved frequently but within a relatively small range, returning time after time to the same locality. They were content to stay within the localized area, depending upon hunting, fishing, and collecting

5

not to scale

Boone Plain Pottery Vessels

vegetable foods. Trading was only with neighboring groups, and the few exotic items such as sea shells were probably the result of innumerable local exchanges before they reached Missouri.

In general the Prairie Forest Potters of the Late Woodland period in the central and western part of Missouri were characterized by the same subsistence practices that supported their Hopewell predecessors, but organizational control of large groups of people to secure their needs and trade their surplus was lacking. Potterymaking continued but the shapes were primarily large, wide-mouthed jars or small bowls of coconut shape without decoration, brushed or covered with cord impressions. Occasionally punctations were added to the rim or vessel lips were notched. The plainness and lack of variety in the pottery easily separates it from the preceding Hopewell and the succeeding village farmers of the Mississippi period.

The Late Woodland period people continued to build mounds to inter their dead, but they were not as well constructed, nor was the grave furniture as elaborate. Very few items were placed with the dead as offerings, and none could be considered outstanding art objects. Typical pipes were made of fired clay rather than of stone and were simple in form. They were of elbow shape rather than the platform base type so distinctive of the Hopewell. The whole life of the people seems to have lacked luster, and except for the larger population and greater distribution they tended to be much more like the earliest pottery makers than any other group. They were also fishermen, as is indicated by their bone fishhooks.

Chipped stone picks and hoes were probably used to dig edible roots,but also may have been the means of mining red ochre and hematite from the huge iron ore deposits at Maramec Spring and near Leslie, Missouri, where aboriginal tunnels were discovered when the modern iron mines were first opened early in the nineteenth century. The Prairie

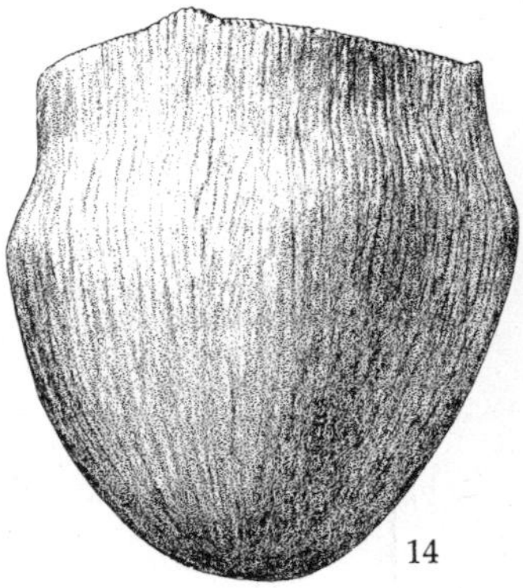

14

Ralls Phase Vessel

4.9

Moreau Cord Marked

Typical Boone Phase Mounds

Forest Potters continued their life style into the Mississippi period, at which time trade was established with the Village Farmers of the great metropolis that had grown up in the region we now call Greater St. Louis.

A distinguishing feature of the Late Woodland period was the appearance for the first time of the bow and arrow. This new invention appears to have been introduced from the west. The larger dart points that had been used to tip the spears thrown with a spear thrower by the Hopewell were still being manufactured and probably were used as arrowheads to a fair extent. Common forms are named *Table Rock Pointed Stem* and *Rice Side Notched*. Perhaps the spear thrower continued in use after the bow and arrow had been accepted as a weapon. Unless we find a dart point hafted on an arrowshaft in some dry cave, we may never know. In any instance the small corner-notched arrowheads, called *Scallorn Corner Notched*, soon became a diagnostic form of the Prairie Forest Potters in this late period. Whenever they are found on a site, pottery is almost certain to be there as well.

It is probably coincidence that the introduction of the superior weapon, the bow and arrow, came about the same time as the breakdown of the Hopewell Ceremonial Complex. It has been speculated that the Hopewell were submerged by an aggressive and more secular people, but it is more likely that the change came about through internal rather than external forces. The evidence points to loss of control of the people by the elite, who were apparently the only ones receiving and exchanging the exotic items. No longer were large amounts of art objects placed with the elite dead in huge, elaborate burial structures. Yet the basic subsistence pattern, their means of making a living, was not greatly changed. The cultural loss

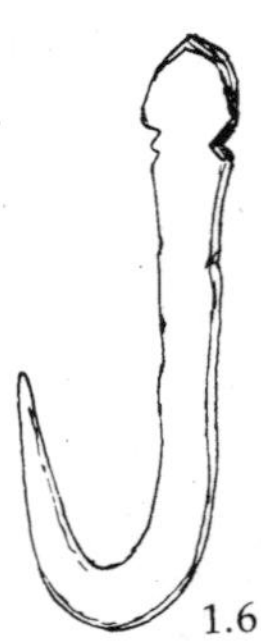

1.6

Bone Fishhook

5.1

Pick

Hoe

Clay Pipe

appears to have been primarily ceremonial activity and trading for exotic materials and the exchange of art objects made from them.

Another change that may have been very important was in gardening. The growing of locally domesticated plants may have continued but corn, the exotic sacred plant imported from the south or southwest, was no longer cultivated. Corn was important to the Hopewell and played a part in their ceremonies, for it has been found as offerings in the mounds for the dead. If corn was an integral part of the trading and exchange ceremonies and those commemorating the dead, its lack concomitant with the changes that occurred suddenly in Hopewell culture may be very significant. A climatic interlude that brought early frosts in both the spring and fall, even if lasting only a few years, could have eliminated the growing of corn in the region. The corn cultivated by the Hopewell would have been fairly recently introduced to the central and northern Mississippi Valley and likely would not have been able to withstand a series of early and late frosts and continue to bear much, if any, crop. If the trading and exchange ceremonies were green corn ceremonies, which continued to be important to Indians living in the eastern United States into the historic period, the inability to grow the ceremonial crop could have been disastrous for the rituals that accompanied the exchanges of exotic materials. Without the corn there could be no corn ceremony.

Whatever the causes, the cultural changes occurring about A.D. 400 and lasting to A.D. 900 are reflected rather dramatically in the archaeological record. The period was long enough for the semipermanent villages of the Prairie Forest Potters to group themselves in certain areas, and strong regional units were formed, which have been given the names *Lindley phase* in the southwestern Ozarks, *Maramec Spring phase* in the central and northern Ozarks, *Randolph phase* in the northwest prairie north of the Missouri River, *Boone phase* and *Ralls phase* in the northeast prairie, *Patrick phase* in the Greater St. Louis vicinity, and *Hoecake phase* in the southeast riverine region of Missouri. Anyone desiring detailed information on these

Rice Side Notched

Table Rock Pointed Stem

Scallorn Corner Notched

phases should refer to the book *Archaeology of Missouri, II.*

The villages that formed the local unions were strong enough that those which did not join in the development of the great Mississippi culture center in the Greater St. Louis area at Cahokia and St. Louis were apparently able to maintain their separateness from the metropolis long after it had colonized most of the upper Mississippi River Valley and areas to the west. There is good evidence that the Late Woodland phase people

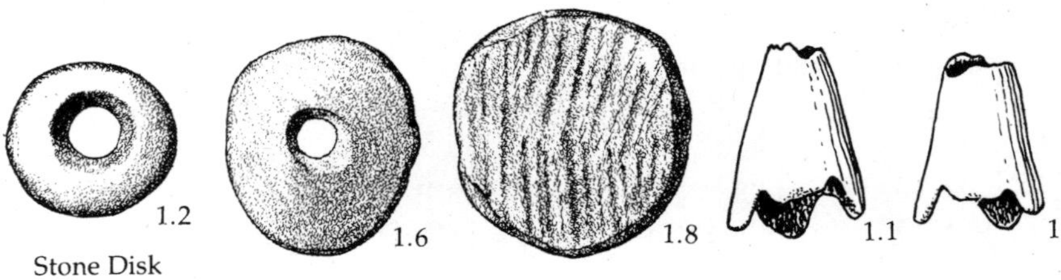

Stone Disk

Pottery Disks

Game Cups

living in the Ozarks and the southeast riverine regions established trade contact with the Village Farmers of the Cahokia–St. Louis vicinity and furnished them with red and yellow ochre for paint, galena for black paint and for making ceremonial objects, and salt for food flavoring.

Perforated pottery disks and small, perforated discoidal-like stone objects may have been used as spindle whorls by the Maramec Spring phase people, thus indicating an emphasis on weaving. Other evidences of weaving are the cord marking and fabric impressions on pottery vessels. Unperforated pottery disks were probably made for gambling. Bone cups used in the very popular Indian cup-and-pin game demonstrate that gambling was an important pastime. Beads and buttons of shell were used for ornaments and decoration of clothing.

A trail, established during the Late Woodland period if not earlier, crossed the Ozark Highland between the Mississippi and Arkansas river drainages. In general it has been replaced today by Interstate Highway 44. The trail was used frequently by hunting and trading parties from the developing metropolis in the Greater St. Louis locality, and evidences of the hunters and traders of the early Mississippi period sometimes are found mixed with or overlying the remains of the Maramec phase people along the trail.

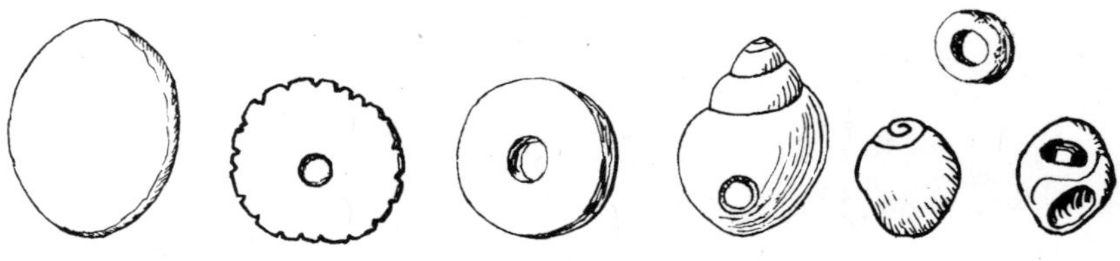

Shell Buttons and Beads natural size

Suggested Reading

Fowler, Melvin L., and Robert L. Hall, 1975. "Archaeological Phases at Cahokia." *Illinois Archaeological Survey Bulletin*, no. 10: 1–14.

Henning, Dale R., 1961. "Archaeological Research in the Proposed Joanna Reservoir, Missouri." *The Missouri Archaeologist* 23: 132–77.

Hopgood, James F., 1969. *An Archaeological Reconnaissance of Portage Open Bay in Southeast Missouri*. Memoir of the Missouri Archaeological Society, no. 7.

Klepinger, Linda, and Dale R. Henning, 1976. "The Hatten Mound, A Two-Component Burial Site in Northeast Missouri." *The Missouri Archaeologist* 37: 92–170.

Martin, Terrell L., 1976. "Prehistoric Settlement-Subsistence Relationships in the Fishing River Drainage, Western Missouri." *The Missouri Archaeologist* 37: 1–91.

Williams, J. Raymond, 1974. "The Baytown Phases in the Cairo Lowland of Southeast Missouri." *The Missouri Archaeologist* 36 (whole volume).

Wood, W. Raymond, 1961. "The Pomme de Terre Reservoir in Western Missouri Prehistory." *The Missouri Archaeologist* 23: 1–131.

Wood, W. Raymond, 1967. "The Fristoe Burial Complex of Southwestern Missouri." *The Missouri Archaeologist* 29 (whole volume).

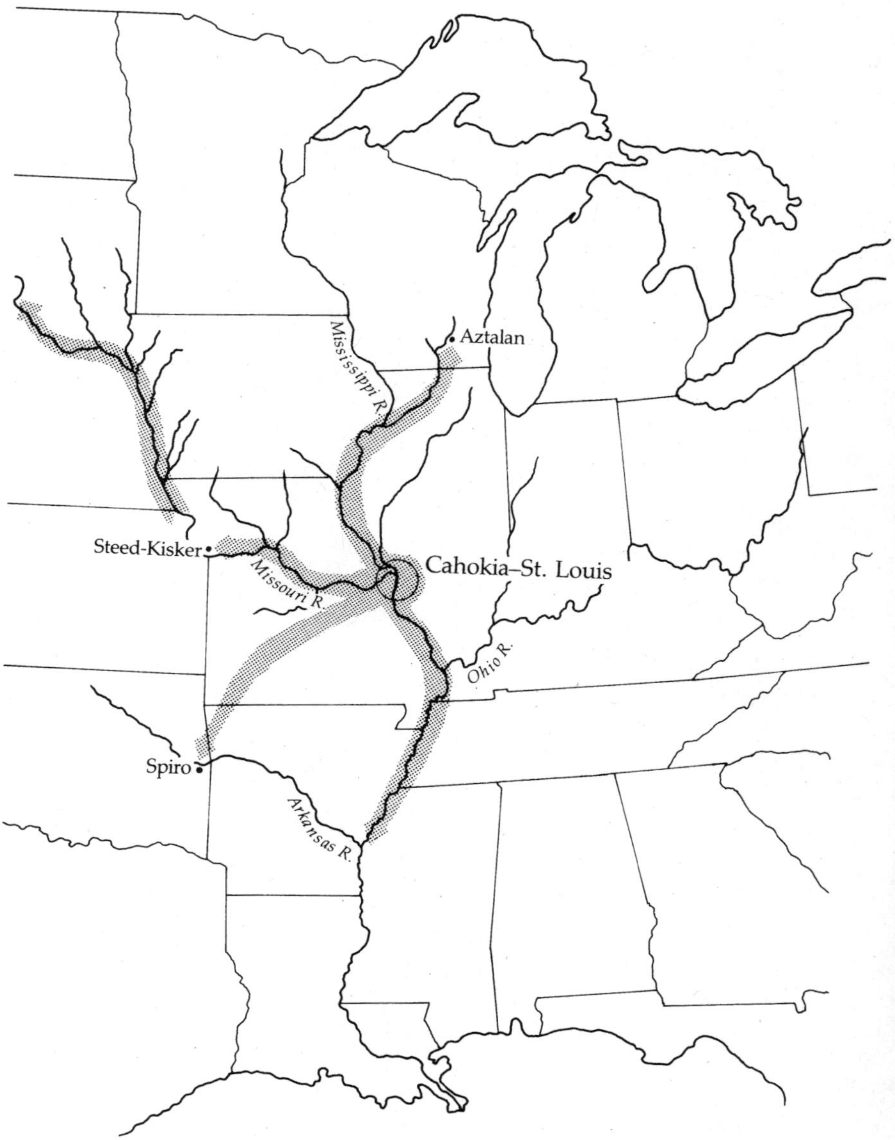

Spread of Mississippi Culture from the Cahokia–St. Louis Center

The Townspeople: Village Farmers of the Mississippi Period

The change from the pattern of living in small villages to that of living in towns was somewhat gradual at the mound metropolis now known as the Greater St. Louis area. The earlier Woodland villages and their culture remained, but were expanded and combined. The resulting amalgamation was fresh and vigorous. A great ceremonial and political center arose—Cahokia–St. Louis. Nearly one thousand years ago the ceremonial center developed into a metropolis which served a series of dependent villages within a radius of thirty to fifty miles and acted as a base for the colonization of much of the upper and central Mississippi River Valley and the lower Missouri Valley. Effects of the center were felt as far south as the mouth of the Arkansas, as far southwest as the Spiro Mound site on the Arkansas River in Oklahoma, and as far northwest as the upper Missouri. There was a secondary center near Kansas City, Missouri, and a migrant colony at Aztalan, Wisconsin. These were migratory moves or intrusions of town dwellers. They introduced a completely new culture, a new way of living, into the areas they penetrated. Archaeologically their cultural remains appear suddenly, without a sequential background of development near Kansas City.

The Mississippi period was characterized by an intrusion of ideas, culture, and people coming from the south, up the Mississippi River Valley. The culture was riverine in type, that is, the settlements and the activities of the people living in them were closely associated with the rivers. The people were dependent upon water-dwelling animals as well as upon river bottomlands suited to agriculture. For the first time in the history of the central Mississippi Valley the Indians were more dependent upon gardening than upon any other activity. Corn, beans, squash, and perhaps a variety of other crops such as sunflowers and gourds were raised intensively by the town dwellers. Fishing was important economically. Another major activity was the collecting of mussels (fresh-water clams) for food and for their shells. Communal hunting was practiced to obtain food for feasts in connection with the ceremonial calendar. Large hunting parties roamed far from the towns, but the towns were not depleted by their absence and continued "business as usual." Smaller hunting parties on a family or clan basis brought in game from the vicinity.

An almost continuous stream of people from the hinterlands brought salt, meat, paint, skins, bow wood, nuts, and other items to barter for goods of equal value or to exchange as presents on a friendly basis. Salt, one of the major trade items, was produced at salt springs not far from the great mound center at St. Louis. Pottery was another item of trade, espe-

10

Ramey Incised

cially the finer wares so distinctive of the Old Village. The jar form called *Ramey Incised,* definitely traded to the Kansas City vicinity and to Aztalan, was a popular trade type. This decorated trade ware became the model for numerous variations that extended into the historic period. Paintstone, red ochre, or hematite was ground to powder and used as body paint as well as for coloring pottery vessels, various objects, altars, and semireligious designs on walls. It was mined in the highland area a few days' journey to the west and must have been brought to the towns by the highland hunter-gatherers. No doubt the townspeople also sent expeditions to obtain such a desired item, visiting the villages or camps of those who dug the ores. Travel was evidently extensive and easy. Large dugout wooden canoes made it possible to traverse the whole length of the Mississippi Valley and to transport goods from one place to another in quantity.

A short distance west of the big center, near present-day Crescent, Missouri, and the Meramec River, was the source of other materials sought after by the town dwellers. The important items were the flint and chalcedony in the hillsides and ridges. Here the townspeople operated open mines to furnish the stone for spades, knives, arrowpoints, and ceremonial blades. They dug holes to expose the flint deposit, which was massive. It has been suggested that a desired block of flint that could not be broken off readily with hammerstones was covered with a thick coating of clay except for the part attaching it to the matrix rock. The rock was heated and then doused with cold water, causing it to crack away from the matrix. The flint was roughed out by percussion and finished by hand-pressure flaking.

Many objects were manufactured in the towns, and one of the most prominent industries was the production of pottery and other clay items. The women made pottery vessels. From the amount of potsherds found on some of the village sites, the women must have spent many hours in the shade of their houses working with pottery clay. Cooking pots were large jars, some of which could be hung over the fire by loop or strap handles attached to the vessel rims. Bowls may also have been used for cooking, but decorations on them and lack of handles suggest that they were what we would call tableware. Plates and smaller vessels were made for mealtime use, and the bean pot was probably an individual dish for stew. Small ladles were also made. Dinnerware included plates and bowls, and water bottles could well have been individual drinking vessels.

Pottery vessels were also fashioned for special needs. A funnel-shaped vessel with openings at both ends has been called a juice press, but may have had some other function such as the leaching of ashes to obtain lye for making hominy. Bowls and water jars for use in religious ceremonies were

7.4

Jar

5.8

6.2

Bowls

decorated with designs thought to be cult symbols. The rim of one specially shaped bowl formed four sets of steps around its perimeter. It is very similar to altar bowls made by the Zuni Indians in the Southwest. The number *four* is sacred to the Zuni and to many other Indian tribes. This sacred number, like our number *seven*, probably has a long history and must have been important to the people of the Mississippi period because many of their cult designs contained four elements. The stepped design was a symbol for rain clouds, and in the case of the Zuni bowl, creatures associated with water were painted on it. The bowl and other items on the altar were intended to aid in bringing rain for the crops of these farming people. It is likely that the Village Farmers in southeast Missouri used the stepped-rim bowls for a similar purpose, as an altar bowl.

Unused and unfired pots were occasionally made to be placed with the dead. Vessels modeled in animal shapes or decorated with modeled

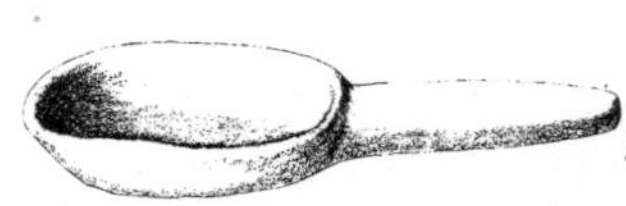

4.8

Ladle

6.9

6.5

Bean Pots

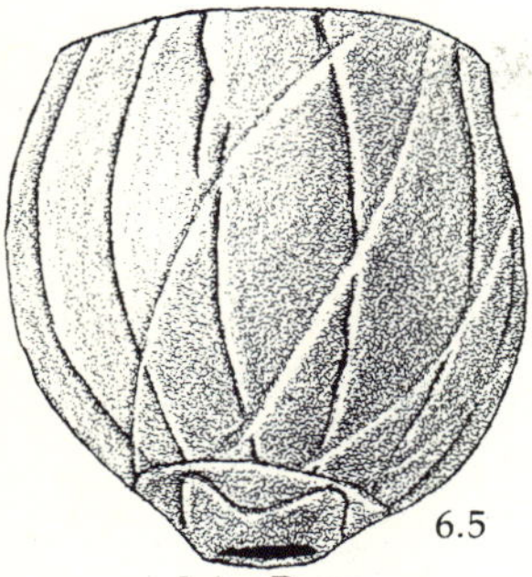

6.5
Juice Press
(Wicliffe Form)

heads, perhaps symbolizing family or clan crests, were also burial offerings. Jars with small openings were for seed storage. Huge, shallow evaporating pans were constructed for making salt.

The townswomen made a fascinating variety of pottery. The shapes range from flattish, unadorned plates and bowls to water bottles that seem like statuettes, they are so fully modeled. A study of the pottery tells much about the life of the people and the animals with which they were familiar—bears, bats, dogs, deer, snakes, turtles, frogs, fish, and birds of all kinds. Some of the animals depicted can only have been the products of a lively imagination, although the recognizable ones are usually quite accurately portrayed. Other vessels represent gourds and shells. Human beings are shown in many ways. In some cases a human head forms the top of a water bottle, and in other instances the whole bottle is in the shape of a head. Such vessels are commonly known as head pots. From them much has been learned about hair styles and face decoration of the townspeople that would never have been known had it not been for the information revealed by the pottery.

Some of the effigy pots portray hunchbacks. The Village Farmers, in common with Indians in other parts of the Americas, held certain physical deformities or abnormalities in awe, perhaps in fear. Myth and story played important parts in such beliefs. Hunchbacks were influential enough to be depicted on the pottery. Cripples and people with deformities often became semireligious leaders or shamans who were believed to have supernatural powers. In one of the towns in Pemiscot County was the grave of a man with a crooked spine and a short, twisted arm. He

Zuni Indian Altar (after Stevenson 1904)

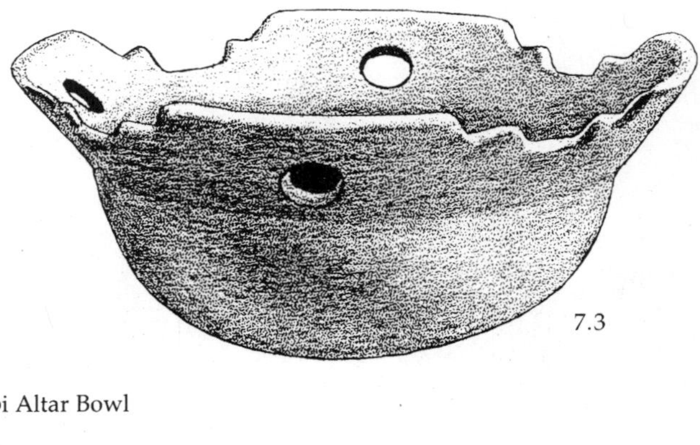

7.3

Mississippi Altar Bowl

6.2

Frog Effigy Jar

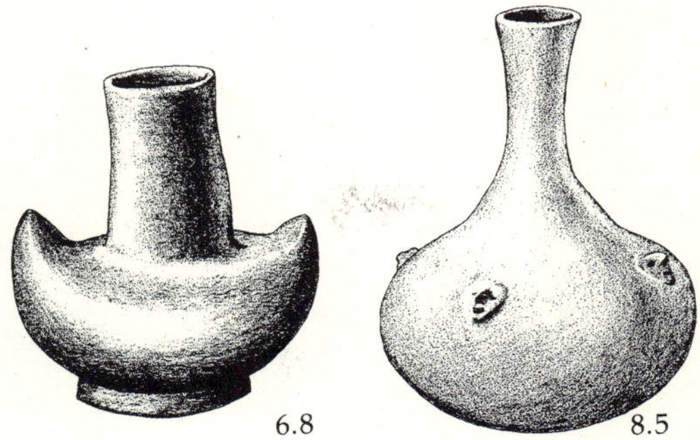

6.8 8.5

Water Bottles

apparently had been feared and respected, for he was buried, not in the town cemetery, but alone, under the floor of the central plaza of the town. This separate burial may have been intended to remove his dangerous spirit from the rest of the dead, or it may have been a means to enable the living of the town to share his power. Both interpretations are debatable.

A small percent of the pottery was painted. Hematite was ground fine and used as pigment. Either the entire vessel was colored, as was the dog effigy bottle found in the grave of the man with the crooked spine, or the red was employed as decoration or design. Another method of pottery ornamentation practiced by the townspeople is known as negative painting. It is achieved by painting the design with a substance that resists taking the color. Thus when the color is applied, only the untreated areas receive it.

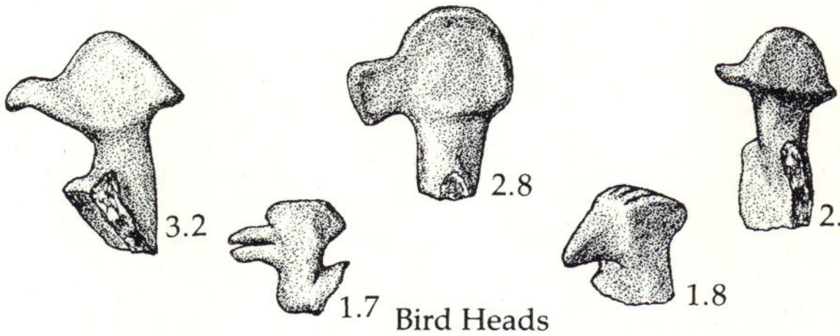

3.2 2.8 2.9 1.7 1.8

Bird Heads

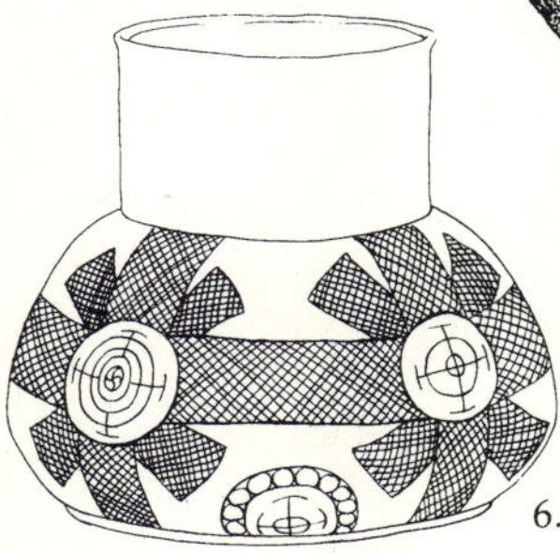

6.1

Cult Vessel

24

Salt Pan

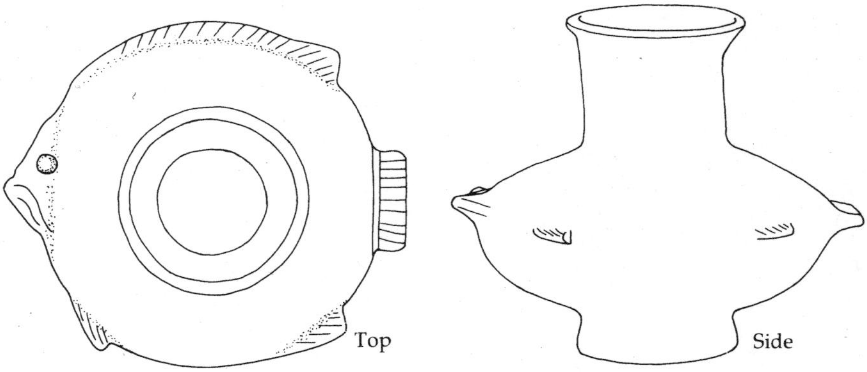

Fish Effigy 6.5

Other fired clay items made by the townspeople were pottery trowels, used for shaping pottery, ear plugs, and pipes. Unusual clay objects such as the Cahokia stumps or boots suggest by their construction and decoration that they must have had a specific use, although we do not yet know what it was.

Stonework is usually not as well represented in the riverine lowlands of the Mississippi Valley as it is in the areas where stone is more plentiful. The manufacture of flaked stone artifacts decreases as the river valley broadens, almost in proportion to the distance from the source of stone of good flaking quality. Near the junction of the Missouri and Mississippi rivers, where an abundance of good stone was being quarried within a short distance of the population center, stonework was important. Arrowheads were made in great quantity and fair variety. Although the side-

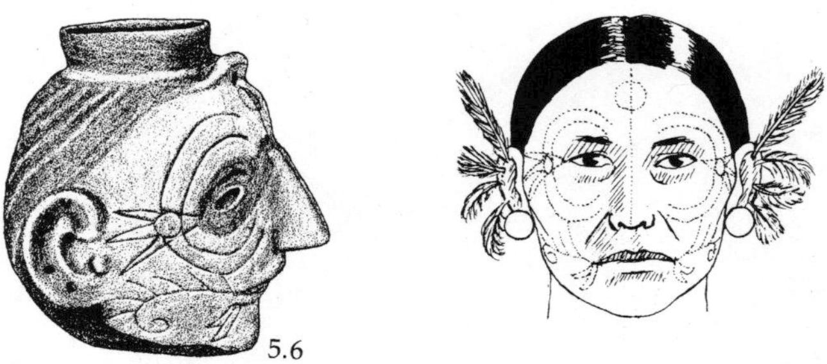

5.6

Head Pot

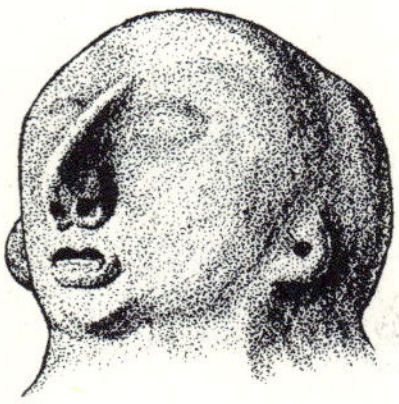

2.8

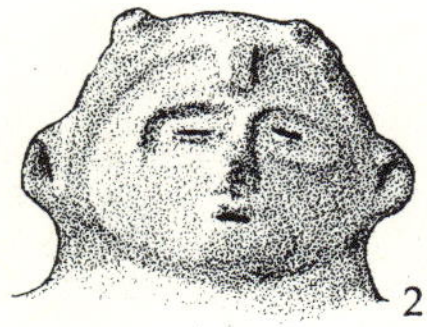

2.7

4.3

Effigy Water Bottle Heads

Hunchback Bottle

notched arrow points have been called *Cahokia Notched*, the most abundant points on the site are the simple triangular forms called *Mississippi Triangular*. Toward the end of the Mississippi Period a willow leaf shaped arrowhead, called *Nodena Elliptical*, became very popular and was a major type found on the Campbell site in the very tip of Missouri's bootheel, relatively close to the Nodena site in Arkansas from which the name was derived.

In addition to arrowheads made by the Village Farmers, the chipped stone items include maces (sometimes depicted in petroglyphs), adzes, notched hoes, and large ovoid spades. The chipped stone indicates a continued interest in hunting and an emphasis on woodworking and digging endeavors. The hoes and spades, although probably cultivating tools as their name suggests, were also used for excavating dirt for building mounds and defensive embankments and for digging house wall trenches and holes for house posts and large ceremonial posts, all of which were major activities in the Village Farmer towns.

8.3

Red Painted Bottle

8

Negative Painted Bottle

The manufacture of stone utilitarian and fine art objects by the process of pecking, grinding, and polishing had reached a point approaching perfection, but was not a major industry. Ceremonial ungrooved axes, called spuds, are examples of the great skill of the stone workers. Large stone pipes were often carved in the shape of a man or a bird. Discoidals were probably used in a ceremonial game similar to one called *chunkey* that was still being played by southeastern Indians in the historic period. Earspools and fluorite beads were made for personal adornment. Stone celts, or ungrooved axes, were used for girdling trees when clearing new fields for farming.

Sharpening stones or whetstones and thin sandstone palettes for final sharpening or polishing are some of the tools used in the manufacture of the stone objects. Hematite appears to have been employed as a polishing medium in conjunction with the thin sandstone polishing slabs that have occasionally been referred to as paint palettes.

The craft of carving bone was not extremely important, but was fairly distinctive. Of special note were the long, decorated bone pins or hair ornaments. A variety of awls and fishhooks were produced. Bone arrowheads were rare.

Antler was more useful than bone in other industries. Antler flaking tools were necessary for flint knapping, and conical antler projectile points were used by some groups as a means of arming their hunting arrows.

Shell was very necessary material in the economy of the riverine townspeople. They fabricated utilitarian items, spoons, scrapers, and hoes from river mussel shells and traded for whelk and conch shells from the Gulf of Mexico. The fact that effigies of the whelk and conch were made in pottery lends support to the assumption that the shell dipper was probably ceremonial in its use. Shells were shaped into disk beads, and the columella—the central or interior column of the shell—was made into beads and pendants. Gorgets, often carved or engraved with figures or designs, have been considered to be ceremonial in nature and are associated with a southeastern ceremonial complex. Shell gorgets and ear plugs of at least

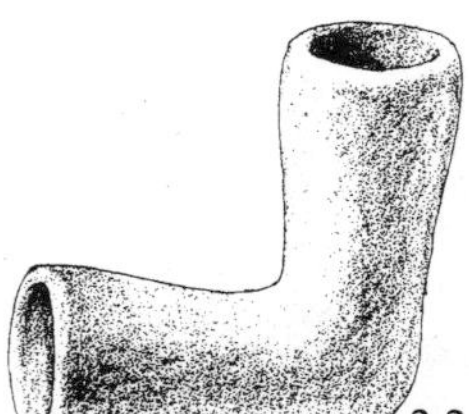
2.2

Clay Pipe

.8

Clay Ear Plug

2.1

Pottery Trowel

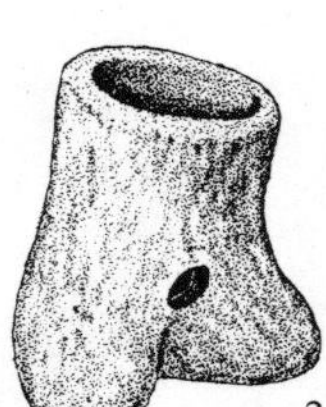
3.5

Cahokia Stump

Cahokia Notched

Mississippi Triangular

Nodena Elliptical

two types have come from the lowland area in southeastern Missouri. Some of them were associated with burials.

Copper was probably sacred to the townspeople, for it is found in the form of ceremonial objects of great esteem. Several embossed copper plaques, undoubtedly some of the rarest artifacts found in Missouri, are the Malden (Wulfing) plates. They are representations of hawks, except for one, which is a hawk with the head of a man.

Copper plaques still held extreme religious significance in the historic period and were revered by southeastern Indian tribes. The plaques seem to have been the most important of all contents of sacred bundles and could be viewed and handled only by irreproachable individuals. They were the holiest of objects, perhaps imbued with impersonal power, representing the welfare and well-being of the community. They were carefully wrapped in deerskin and enclosed in a sacred bundle consisting of a woven mat case or a woven bag.

Cloth, matting, and skins were items associated with copper, and where they were in contact with the plaques, bits of these usually perishable

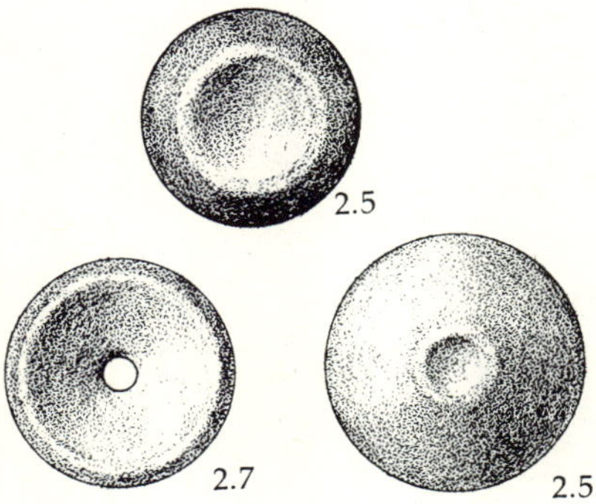

2.5 2.7 2.5

Discoidals

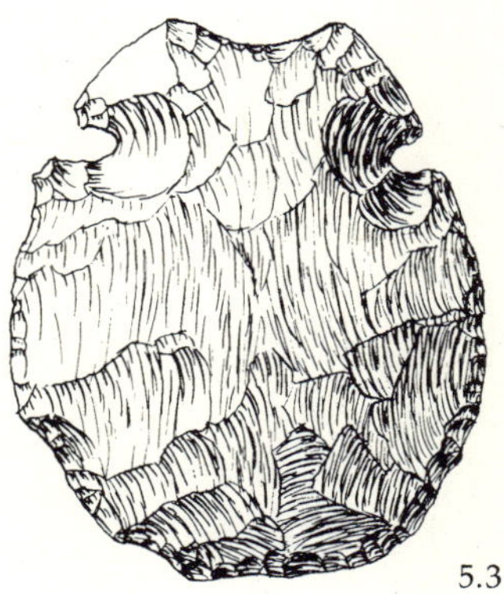

5.3

Notched Hoe

objects have been preserved by the copper salts. Wood was also preserved when covered by a thin layer of copper.

Early European travelers who visited villages similar in culture to the Middle Mississippi town dwellers of Missouri wrote of the temples with carved wooden posts standing up from the roofs and wooden idols inside. Large posts with faces carved on the tops were set up in a ring in the village and were the focal point of dances during feasts. Wooden masks and statuettes, both animal and human, rattles, plaques, and other objects from similar cultures in other states have been preserved by favorable conditions, but unfortunately very few wooden objects made by the townspeople have survived in Missouri. No doubt wood was used for boats, bows, mortars and pestles, bowls, houses, defenses, decorated posts in the town squares, and for an infinite number of other useful and ornamental things, including decoration on the temples and the houses of the dead.

The woodworker's tools were razor sharp. A man who lived in one of the southeastern towns must have been an especially fine wood-carver, for when he died his stone adzes were buried with him. They were beautifully made and had been freshly sharpened before being placed in the grave. They would have been a fine legacy for an heir or an apprentice, but the fact that they were interred raises the interesting speculations that the adzes had been dedicated to the carving of sacred objects and as such must not be used again, or that the wood-carver himself was so expert that his

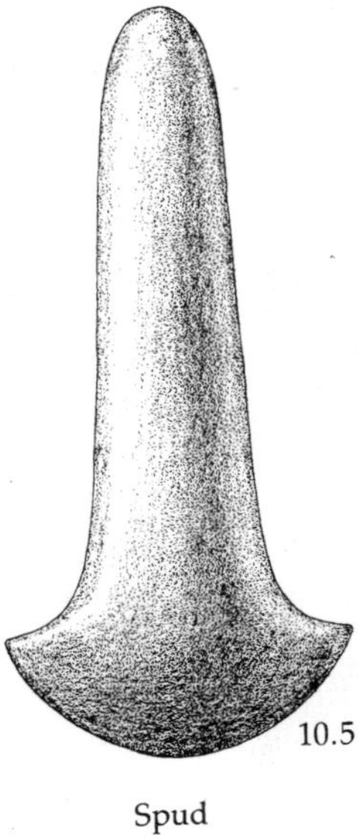

10.5

Spud

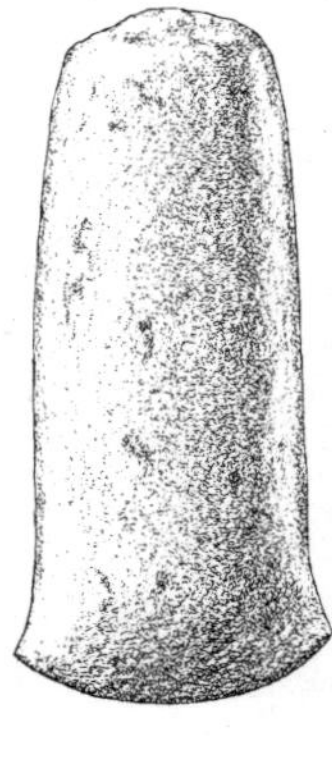

6.3

Celt

9.2

Spade

.5

Marginella Bead

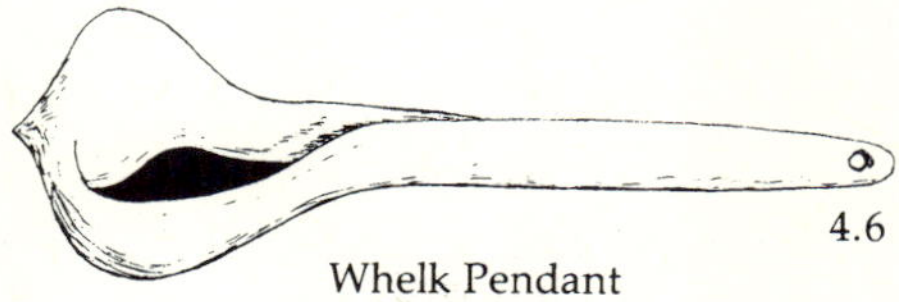
4.6

Whelk Pendant

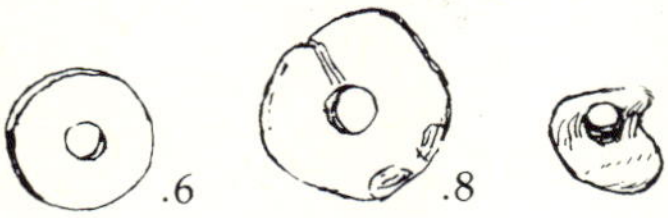
.6 .8 .5

Disk Beads

2.7

Conch Columella Bead

tools were too fine to be profaned by less worthy hands. For whatever reason, the implements were not allowed to outlast the man in whose grave they were found.

The few wooden objects which have come to light in Missouri are a boat, bows, and the backing for copper ceremonial ornaments. The boat was preserved under water in a cave in southeastern Missouri; it had been carved from a single log. It was thirty feet long and approximately eighteen inches wide. Bows have come from dry shelters in southwestern Missouri and from a mound. The lack of stone mortars or metates is a certain indication that mortars and pestles of wood were employed by a people who needed to grind their corn in some manner.

Houses were square, rectangular, or round and had wooden frameworks and thatched roofs. Some had two to five center posts, and other,

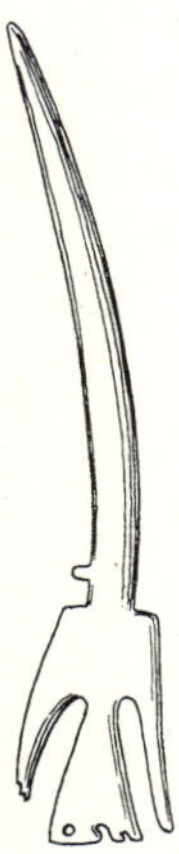
8.7

Bone Pin

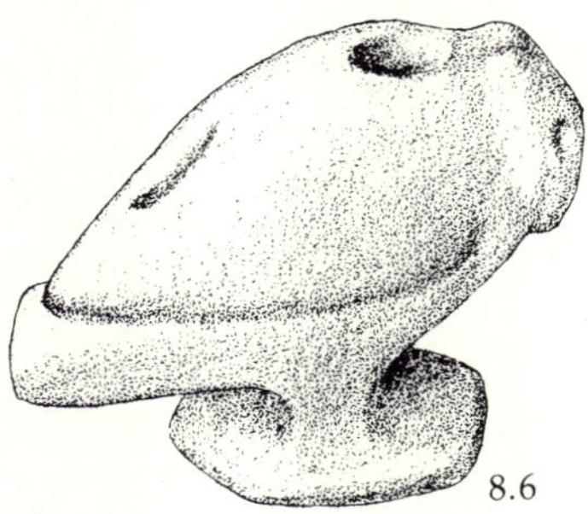
8.6

Stone Owl Effigy Pipe

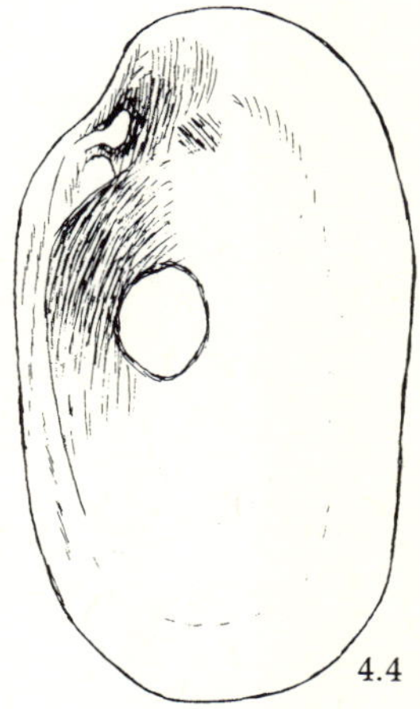
4.4

Shell Hoe

5.4

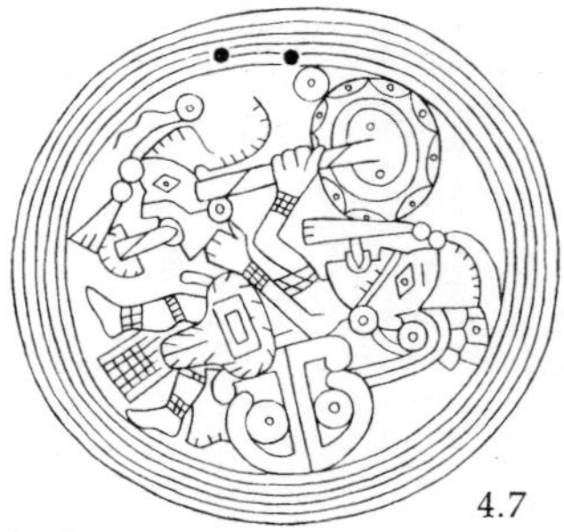
4.7

Shell Gorgets

smaller houses had one, two, or no center posts at all. The small houses had sunken floors and wall trenches with small posts in the trenches. The wall trenches did not meet at the corners, although the walls no doubt did. The larger houses with two to five center posts did not have wall trenches; the posts were set directly into the floor. In Mississippi, New Madrid, and Scott counties, Missouri, houses had five center posts and a double wall of small posts supporting a wall of wattle and daub. A palisade consisting of a double wall of posts was implanted on top of an embankment opposite a ditch which surrounded the village.

Each major town usually contained a temple mound, which may also have held on its top the house of the dead, and a chief's mound on which stood the chief's house. The mounds were large and flat topped, to serve as bases for the buildings. Some villages had an arrangement of the mounds around a plaza.

Burials were in cemeteries at particular spots within the general village area. As a rule the burial was in a grave eighteen to forty-two inches deep, but sometimes the body was placed on the ground and covered with dirt, which resulted in the cemetery area gradually becoming a mound. There is some evidence that clans had separate burial plots and that the families within the clans were assigned places within the plots.

Burials were usually made in the flesh, with the body placed on its back. Generally, though not always, burial goods accompanied the dead. Nor-

2.9

4.5

Shell Gorgets

15

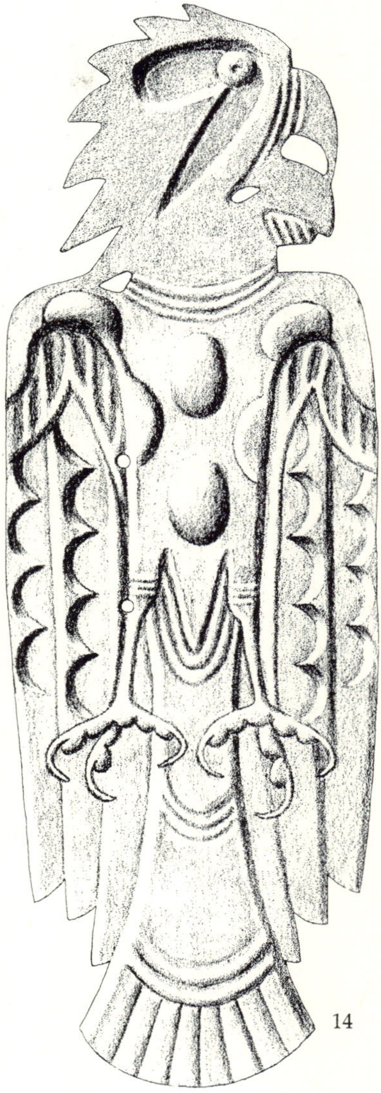

14

Copper Plaques
Malden Plates
(Lower Edges Reconstructed)

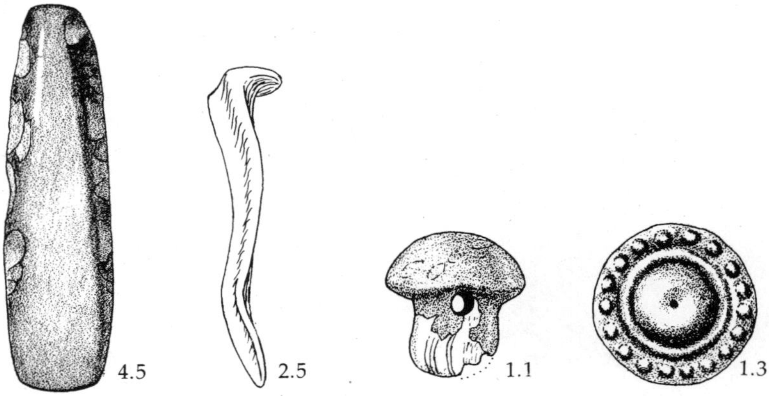

Stone Adz   Shell Ear Plugs   Copper Ear Ornament

mally, grave offerings were vessels of food and water and the ornaments or special tools of the deceased. Some burials were secondary, especially those of the most important personages. The body was exposed, and then the bones were picked clean, wrapped in a bundle, and buried. Sometimes in the secondary burial the skull was placed on top or between the crossed leg bones. The skull-and-bones death symbol was in common use by the Indians as far south as Mexico, where it was observed by the Spanish in the historic period. The *skull-and-cross-bones* on the pirate flag and on poison labels is derived from the Indian symbols.

The Indians of the Mississippi period participated in a religious cult that

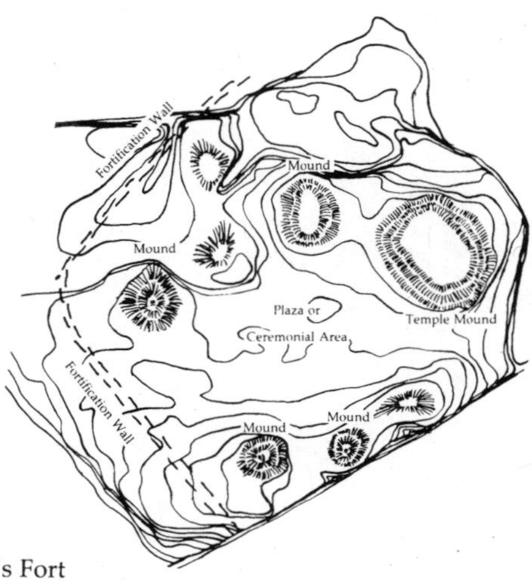

Old Map of Beckwith's Fort
(after Thomas, 1884)

Pottery Design, Alabama

Bas Relief, Mexico

had numerous symbols associated with it. They included crosses, maces or batons, bilobed arrows, hands, weeping eyes, sunbursts, snakes, and birds. The symbols were placed on sacred objects and at venerated places. An outstanding example of the carving of cult symbols on rocks, a petroglyph site, has been preserved by the Missouri State Park Board in Washington State Park, Washington County, Missouri.

The Washington State Park petroglyph site was probably the junction of game trails and war trails, and was possibly a consecrated spot where young men were initiated into secret society rites and were taught the mythology associated with the initiation. The rock carvings may have been memory aids for songs and rites that were part of the ceremony. The symbols probably had magical as well as religious meaning, and participation in the ceremonies at the sacred spot could have been the means of imparting the powers of the symbols to the participants.

The Village Farmers in the Mississippi period, A.D. 900–1700, displayed a great deal of variation, partly due to the long time span during which their culture existed, and partly due to the physiographic areas represented within Missouri and their effect upon the spread of the ideas and culture of the time.

Reconstruction of Beckwith's Fort

Suggested Reading

Chapman, Carl H., compiler, 1977. "Investigation and Comparison of Two Fortified Mississippi Tradition Archaeological Sites in Southeastern Missouri: A Preliminary Compilation." *The Missouri Archaeologist* 38 (whole volume).

Chapman, Carl H., 1976. "Internal Settlement Designs of Two Mississippian Tradition Ceremonial Centers in Southeastern Missouri." In *Cultural Change and Continuity: Essays in Honor of James Bennett Griffin*, edited by Charles E. Cleland, pp. 121–46, Academic Press, New York.

Fowler, Melvin L., 1969. *Explorations into Cahokia Archaeology*. Illinois Archaeological Survey, Inc., Bulletin no. 7, University of Illinois, Urbana.

Fundaburk, Emma Lila, and Mary Douglas Foreman, 1957. *Sun Circles and Human Hands*. Luverne, Alabama.

Hamilton, Henry W., 1952 (reprinted 1981). "The Spiro Mound." *The Missouri Archaeologist* 14 (whole volume).

Hamilton, Henry W., Jean Tyree Hamilton, and Eleanor F. Chapman, 1974. *Spiro Mound Copper*. Missouri Archaeological Society Memoir, no. 11.

Howard, James H., 1968. *The Southeastern Ceremonial Complex*. Missouri Archaeological Society Memoir, no. 6.

Illinois Archaeological Survey, 1975. *Perspectives in Cahokia Archaeology*. Bulletin no. 10, University of Illinois, Urbana.

Keslin, Richard O., 1964. "Archaeological Implications on the Role of Salt as an Element of Cultural Diffusion." *The Missouri Archaeologist* 26 (whole volume).

Klippel, Walter E., 1969. "The Hearnes Site: A Multi-Component Occupation Site and Cemetery in the Cairo Lowland Region of Southeast Missouri." *The Missouri Archaeologist* 31 (whole volume).

Phillips, Philip, 1970. *Archaeological Survey in the Lower Yazoo Basin, Mississippi, 1949–1955* (in two parts). Papers of the Peabody Museum of Archaeology and Ethnology, Harvard University, 25, Cambridge.

Price, James E., and James B. Griffin, 1979. *The Snodgrass Site of the Powers Phase of Southeast Missouri*. Anthropological Papers, Museum of Anthropology, University of Michigan, no. 66.

Shippee, J. M., 1972. *Archaeological Remains in the Kansas City Area: The Mississippian Occupation*. Missouri Archaeological Society Research Series, no. 9.

Smith, Bruce D., 1978. *Prehistoric Pattern of Human Behavior: A Case Study in the Mississippi Valley*. Academic Press, New York.

The Prairie Dwellers: Protohistoric Period

The introduction of a new element into the American scene about the turn of the sixteenth century (A.D. 1500) soon sent its influence up and down the Mississippi Valley. In 1540 Hernando de Soto penetrated to the Arkansas River and perhaps well into southeastern Missouri. It may never be known how much De Soto and his cruel army affected the Indians living in what is now northern Arkansas and southern Missouri, but it seems probable that part of the rapid decline of the townspeople after De Soto's appearance in A.D. 1540 can be laid indirectly, if not directly, at his feet. De Soto brought immediate change in the existing provinces controlled by great towns by deposing the town leaders indiscriminately. But a more far-reaching effect was the introduction of European diseases, which occasioned alarm in the Indians that could not be dispelled. Uncompromising fears and flight to hinterland areas by family and clan groups may have completed the breakdown of the great towns that was begun by the violence and disruption attending De Soto's angry march. Priest and shaman attempting to exorcise the new disease devils were themselves possessed and consumed. Systems of trade, protective agreements with neighbors, the integrated divisions of labor effecting a well-balanced and efficient supply of food—all disintegrated, adding to the chaos. The great towns were abandoned or reduced and disorganized.

In early historic times the Quapaw, a large tribe, lived in three towns near the mouth of the Arkansas River. They may have been prairie Indians who had not been in the area long. They were closely related to the Dhegiha Siouan-speaking Osage, Omaha, Kansas, and Ponca, who were typically prairie-oriented in cultural development. Possibly the Quapaw moved into the area from the north and west, filling a population vacuum and picking up some of the cultural background of the great towns as well as amalgamating with the remnants of the townspeople. Another interpretation, perhaps more feasible, is that the Quapaw were some of the remnants who remained in their old towns and salvaged much of their old culture while their brothers and sisters dispersed to the prairies and reassembled into the tribes of history known as the Osage, Kansas, and Omaha. It does appear that the Osage, Kansas, and Omaha formed as separate tribal units after A.D. 1500. Much of their ethnographic background is related to and perhaps derived from the culture developed in the southeastern lowland area. At this time the full and certain story of the development of the historic tribes is yet to be written.

There is some evidence that the Osage originated from diverse units in Arkansas, Missouri, Oklahoma, and Kansas, as no definite sequential Osage development can be found in the four-state area; no antecedent

10

Cooking Jar

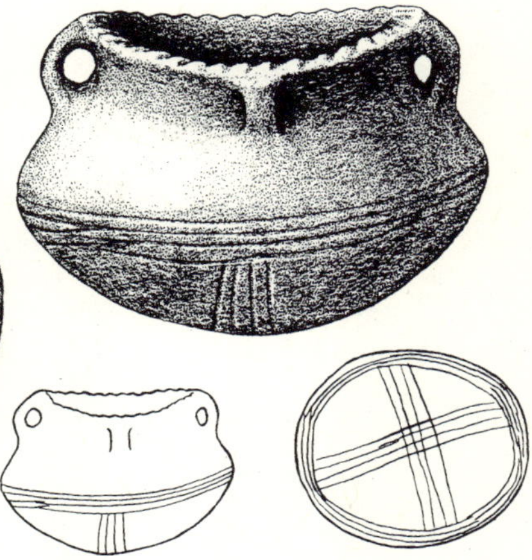

Funeral Vessel 3.3

large sites that would be the basis of the Osage development have been located. The sites that seem most closely related culturally to historic Osage sites are small, representing little units such as a family or clan and related in part to the southeastern cultural development. No documented villages have been reported of any of the Dhegiha Sioux except the Quapaw prior to A.D. 1700.

The great St. Louis-Cahokia center at the junction of the Missouri and Mississippi rivers may have been too far north to have suffered serious disrupting influences from the De Soto invasion. On the other hand it is probable that the center deteriorated long before the time of De Soto's expedition. The evidence is not clear on this point. It does not seem likely that the Illinois tribes found there in the historic period were representative of the earlier cultural development. The Illinois cultural development more nearly equates with that of the Osage, and the Illinois tribes probably entered the area in late prehistoric times.

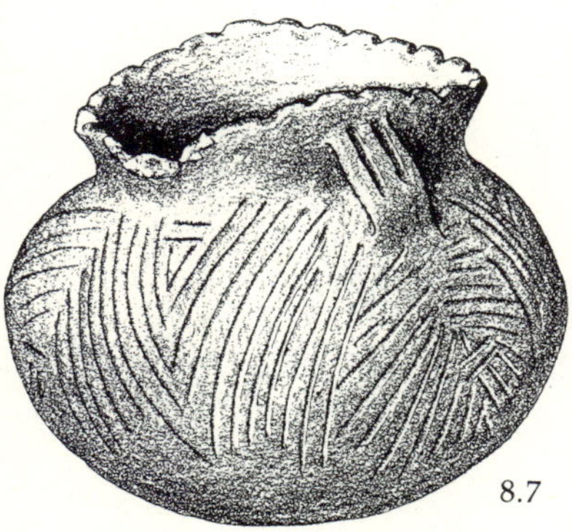

8.7

Elliptical Vessel (Van Meter Trailed)

Cahokia appears to have been a hearth of culture during the early Mississippi period and perhaps continued to influence the growth of a cultural development called *Oneota*. As the Oneota developed, Cahokia may have declined. At any rate, by the beginning of the Protohistoric period, the Oneota culture had become separate and distinct, and by the beginning of the Historic period in A.D. 1673, the mounds at St. Louis were the only evidence of

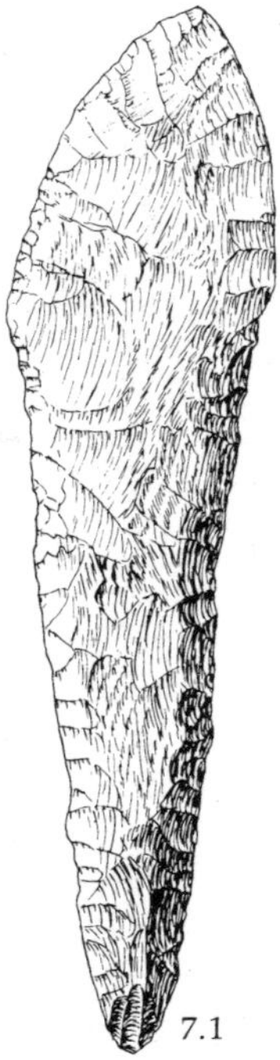
7.1

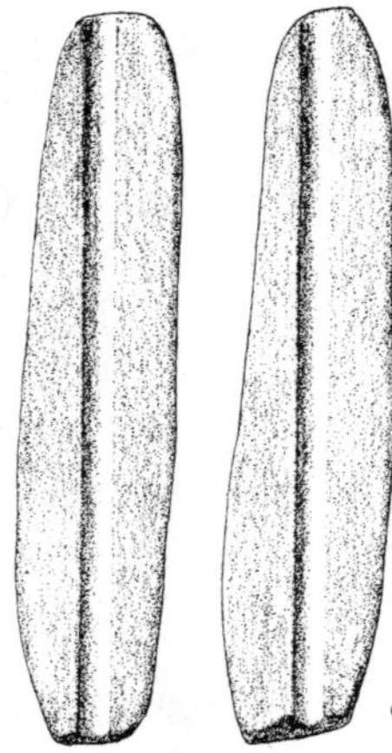
9

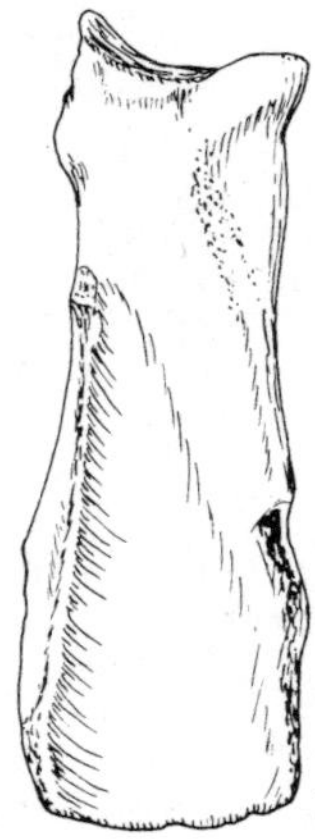
12.9

Knife | Paired Arrowshaft Smoothers | Bison Scapula Hoe

the flourishing city that had existed there earlier.

Oneota was a general cultural growth, probably stimulated by the Cahokia center. The area in which it developed can be bounded by lines drawn from St. Louis to Kansas City, due north to the Minnesota River, east to Aztalan, and south to Cahokia at East St. Louis. The story concerning the spread of the Oneota people over this area is not entirely clear. When the Oneota people moved to the mouth of the Grand River in central Missouri

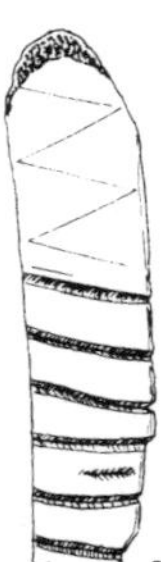
3.7

5.4

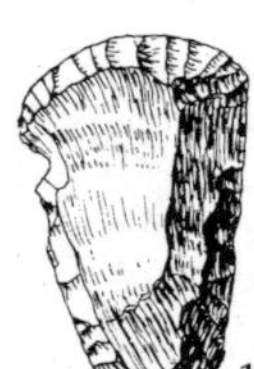
1.9

2

Bone Tally | Bone Awl | Scraper | Pipe Drill

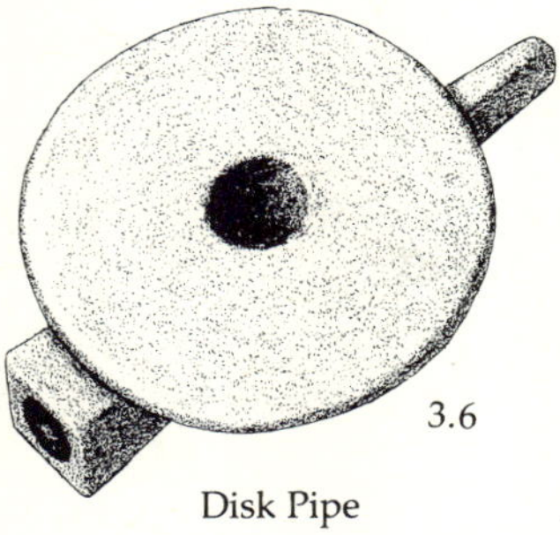

3.6

Disk Pipe

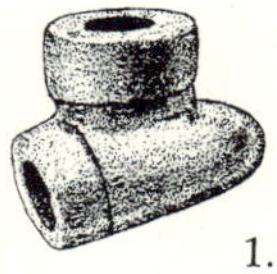

1.2

Elbow Pipe

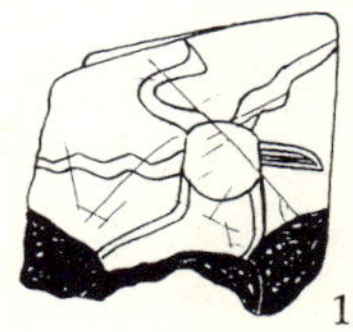

1.5

Catlinite Engraved Tablet

about A.D. 1350, they had a full-blown Oneota culture; no antecedents from which they might have developed existed there.

The Oneota people in central Missouri are represented by only a few sites, many of which are south of the Missouri River. Most prominent is the Utz site, which is the location of the Missouri Indian village prehistorically as well as historically. The Missouri Indians in the Protohistoric period had a rich and varied Oneota culture.

The protohistoric Missouri Indian women manufactured pottery vessels of several varieties, but the jar is the most common shape, typically high rimmed with vertical grooves or trailed lines and/or thumb impressions, usually with two handles though sometimes four. Another type is a large low-rimmed jar that is decorated in several styles, and a third is a plain ware, occasionally without handles. These were used as cooking pots. The fourth main type is a smaller, highly decorated vessel—perhaps for personal use—which frequently is elliptical in shape. Two minor types are miniature vessels that have been found associated with burials as funeral offerings, and deep, straight-sided bowls.

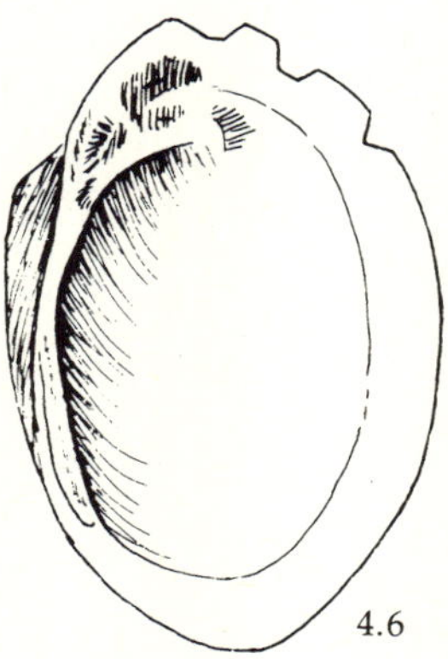

4.6

Shell Spoon

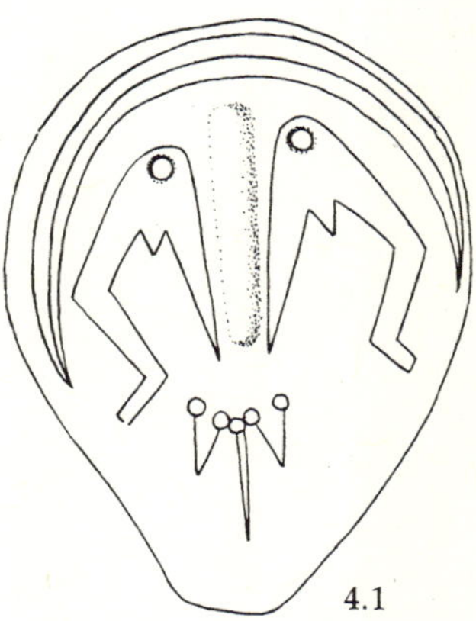

4.1

Mask Gorget

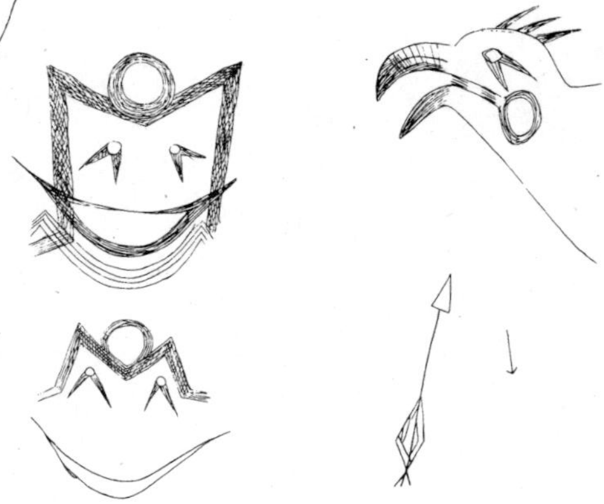

The Jim Utz Catlinite
Engraved Tablet

Design Elements

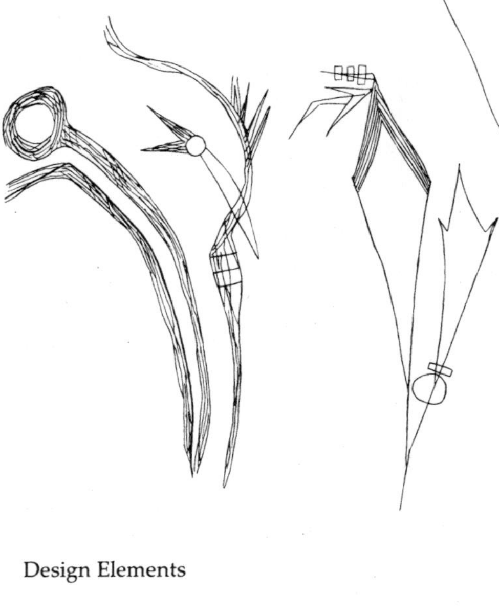

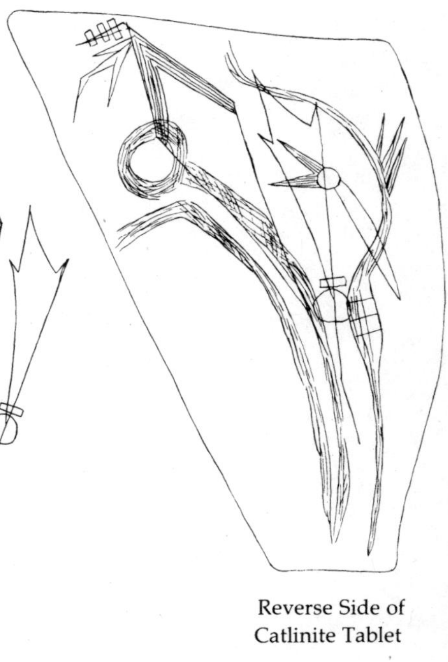

Design Elements

Reverse Side of
Catlinite Tablet

A fine quality of pottery clay is available in the deep ravines near the hilltop village site, and it probably was used in making the pottery vessels. All the pottery is shell tempered. Large flakes of shell are visible on larger jars, and the tempering was very liberally added to the paste. There is a tendency for some of the pottery to flake off or to shatter into horizontal flakes.

The men manufactured stone tools and weapons by the chipping process. Stonework is typified by the simple, triangular arrowhead, flake end scraper, beveled knife, elliptical knife, handled knife, large ceremonial knife, and pipe drill. Excellent stone for the chipped stone artifacts was available in the glacial deposits at the edges of the Utz site.

The Oneota (protohistoric Missouri Indians) were hunters, fishers, gardeners, and gatherers of wild food plants. They hunted with bow and arrow, the arrowshafts shaped by pairs of grooved sandstone tools. Their prowess at hunting is evidenced by the large number of animal bones in the trash pits of the village. Deer was the animal most frequently taken in the hunt, and turkey and waterfowl perhaps ranked next. Bison and elk furnished meat and hides, but few bones of these large animals were brought back from the hunting trips. Bison shoulder blades were selected to be used as hoes, and ribs to be made into arrowshaft straighteners, tallies, and mat-weaving needles. Elk antlers were brought back to be fashioned into handles. Deer, turkey, and waterfowl bones provided the material for awls, fish gorges, and cylindrical beads.

Fishing in the cutoff lakes and in the Missouri River supplied the Missouri Oneota people with a ready source of food. Fish bones and scales are plentiful in the trash preserved by wood ashes in refuse pits. Turtles were taken in great numbers, and mussels were collected by the thousands. The mussels must have furnished part of the diet, and their shells yielded tempering material for pottery making. Many shells, the edges notched, were used as spoons.

The Oneota made special ornaments of sea shells that had come through trade channels from the Gulf of Mexico; they used the large conch shells to make columella beads and disk beads. Decorated mask gorgets and ear pendants were also cut from conch shells, and all the special ornaments must have been displayed on significant occasions. The face-mask gorget was worn on the chest, or at the throat.

The most characteristic ceremonial items of the protohistoric Missouri Indian were the catlinite engraved tablets. The catlinite had to be obtained from the pipestone quarry in Minnesota, now preserved in Pipestone National Monument. Catlinite tablets were engraved with symbols similar to those used by the townspeople of the preceding period. The forked-eye design, a prominent cult symbol of the southeastern townspeople, was depicted on both the catlinite tablets and the shell-mask gorgets.

Pipes were also made of red pipestone or catlinite, and a common form smoked by the Missouri was a disk bowl shape. Variations of elbow pipes were also used. The pipes and the catlinite tablets were no doubt featured in special ceremonies in connection with the use of sacred plants, among which was tobacco. Pipes were a means by which the incense of the tobacco plant could be offered to the mysterious powers of the sun, the moon, the thunder, and the winds of the four directions.

The life of the Oneota people included hunting trips far to the west for bison and other game. Large bell-shaped storage pits were dug deep in the ground for storing valuables and food supplies while the families followed the chase. These same pits became receptacles for trash that accumulated near the fireplaces or on house floors. Cache pits, dug with hoes made of bison scapula bones, were sometimes as much as eleven feet deep and six feet in diameter at the bottom.

Cultivation of corn, beans, and squash supplemented the plentiful meat diet. Nuts and seeds were gathered and then pounded with a grooved maul into meal to add as flavoring or thickening to stew.

The protohistoric Oneota blends into the historic Missouri Indian culture. At present it is not possible to separate the protohistoric culture from the historic except on an arbitrary basis, but the separation will be

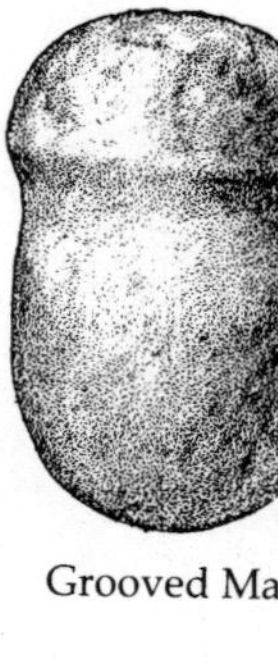

5.5
Grooved Maul

possible as more study is made of the Utz Site and surrounding Oneota sites in the state of Missouri.

Suggested Reading

Bray, Robert T., 1963. "Southern Cult Motifs from the Utz Oneota Site, Saline County, Missouri." *The Missouri Archaeologist* 25: 1–40.

Bray, Robert T., 1978. "European Trade Goods from the Utz Site and the Search for Fort Orleans." *The Missouri Archaeologist* 39: 1–75.

Brose, David S., 1978. "Late Prehistory of the Upper Great Lakes Area." In *Handbook of North American Indians, Northeast,* edited by Bruce G. Trigger, 15: 569–82, U.S. Government Printing Office, Washington, D.C.

Gibbon, Guy E., 1972. "Cultural Dynamics and the Development of the Oneota Life-Ways in Wisconsin." *American Antiquity* 37(2): 166–85.

Glenn, Elizabeth J., 1974. *Physical Affiliations of the Oneota People.* University of Iowa Press, Iowa City.

Griffin, James B., 1960. "A Hypothesis for the Prehistory of the Winnebago." In *Culture in History,* edited by Stanley Diamond, Columbia University Press, New York.

Hamilton, Henry W., 1967. *Tobacco Pipes of the Missouri Indians.* Memoir of the Missouri Archaeological Society, no. 5.

Harvey, Amy E., 1979. *Oneota Culture in Northwestern Iowa.* University of Iowa Press, Iowa City.

Henning, Dale R., 1970. "Development and Interrelationships of Oneota Culture in the Lower Missouri River Valley." *The Missouri Archaeologist* 32 (whole volume).

McKusick, Marshall, 1973. *The Grant Oneota Village.* University of Iowa Press, Iowa City.

Mason, Carol I., 1976. "Historic Identification and Lake Winnebago Focus Oneota." In *Culture Change and Continuity: Essays in Honor of James Bennett Griffin,* edited by Charles E. Cleland, pp. 335–48, Academic Press, New York.

Straffin, Dean, 1971. *The Kingston Oneota Site.* University of Iowa Press, Iowa City.

Wedel, Mildred Mott, 1959. "The Oneota Sites on the Upper Iowa River." *The Missouri Archaeologist* 21(2–4): 1–181.

Wedel, Waldo R., 1959. *An Introduction to Kansas Archaeology.* Smithsonian Institution, Bureau of American Ethnology, Bulletin 174, U.S. Government Printing Office, Washington, D.C.

The Missouri and Osage: Indians of History

The exact time that the Missouri tribe first met the French is not known. The meeting probably took place at the Missouri village located on the Pinnacles, now in Van Meter State Park near Miami, Missouri. The first recorded meeting was before 1720, and the man recording it was Bourgmont, who had gone to the village about 1714. Bourgmont was well received not only by the Missouri but also by the Osage and induced the little Osage to break away from the Big Osage and establish themselves near the Missouri Indian village to take advantage of the trade he promised them. A map drawn sometime between 1723 and 1728 shows the locations of both villages.

The Little Osage moved near the Missouri village, and in 1723 Bourgmont established Fort Orleans, essentially a trading post, on the north side of the Missouri River, which at that time apparently ran south of its present course. Thus began an intensive fur and hide trade with the Missouri tribe, who moved their village upstream a few miles to be closer to Fort Orleans. After 1763, until they left what is now the state of Missouri to join the Oto in Nebraska in the latter part of the eighteenth century, the Missouri were seemingly less powerful than the Osage, and when the final move was made several families joined the Osage when they returned to their homeland on the upper Osage River about 1790. The Missouri were closely related to the Iowa, Oto, and Winnebago linguistically; all four tribes spoke the Chiwere Sioux language. It is understandable that most of the Missouri tribe amalgamated with the Oto rather than the Osage, who spoke another Siouan language, the Dhegiha Sioux.

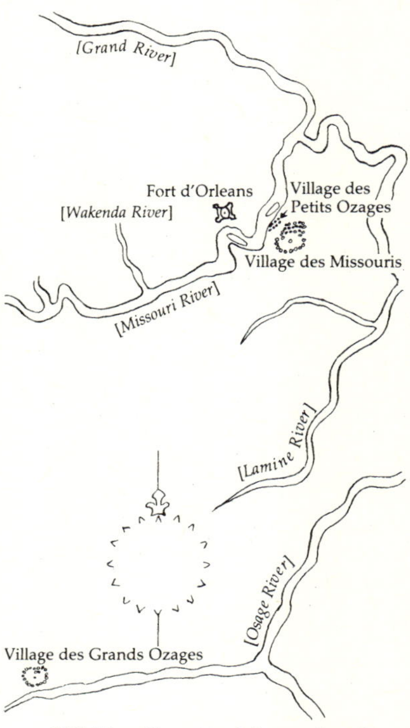

Old Map Showing Missouri and Osage Villages

The Missouri tribe in the Protohistoric period was typically Oneota in culture. Missouri Indian culture remained much as it had been in the Protohistoric period. Additions were

primarily trade ornaments consisting of Venetian blue glass beads, copper and brass rings, bracelets, cylindrical beads, and conical tinklers. Kettles of brass or copper and knives of iron seem to have been the only French trade items of utilitarian nature.

Missouri Indian villages were relatively large; the Utz site encompassed from 150 to 300 acres. How much of the site was used at any one time is not known, but at the very least it must have included 30 to 40 acres. The site was a permanent base from which hunting excursions were made far enough west to obtain buffalo. Deer and elk abounded in the surrounding prairies; the remains of deer are the main bone refuse on the site. Turkey and duck bones are plentiful, and fish and turtle bones indicate an additional dependence upon water animals for food.

The Missouri Indians gathered wild food and were especially fond of the American lotus (*Nelumbo lutea*) seeds and roots. The women, young and old, dug the lily roots from the shallow lakes, using long, pointed poles. Much ceremony accompanied the collecting of the first root, and part of it was carefully returned to the water. The gathering was an occasion of gaiety and frolic. Reeds, growing at the edges of lakes filled with water lilies, were woven into mats, useful household items of furniture as well as covering for the houses.

Gardening was important, and corn, beans, and squash were vegetable staples. Just where the gardens were in relation to the village is not known, but probably they were in the lowland of Muddy Creek south and east and in the Missouri River bottomland at the foot of the Pinnacles to the west.

Most excavations have been conducted in small areas due to the limitation of time and to the richness and depth of the deposits. One of the largest single digs was an area approximately thirty by forty feet; within it were forty pits, many of which had cut through earlier pits. They were in a line paralleling the crown of the ridge. Recent excavations have revealed house evidences consisting of postmolds in an elliptical pattern and enclosing fire hearths and large bell-shaped storage pits. The Missouri houses were of the prairie lodge type similar to those of the Iowa and Osage, built of a framework of poles and covered with woven mats.

All of the items described previously, except for French trade goods, are things that the Missouri Indians had and used when they first met the French. The tribe was numerous and powerful, the first and strongest to be met when traveling up the Missouri River. They gave their name to the river, then to the territory, and eventually to the state. The village site where the French first encountered them has been preserved in Van Meter State Park by the Missouri State Park Board; the University of Missouri in cooperation with the Missouri State Park Board is continuing the study of the old village and is interpreting the evidences for the future benefit of Missourians.

The Osage may have been in southwestern Missouri in 1673 when the discoverers of the Mississippi River, Louis Jolliet and Father Jacques Marquette, learned about them from other Indians. At least they were organized as a tribe by that time and were located south of the Missouri River. At approximately A.D. 1700 the Osage were in Vernon County, Missouri, on the south side of the Osage River. The first recorded visit to them by the French was in 1719 when Du Tisne noted that he had been in their village on the Osage River. Just prior to 1719, one group of Osage, the Little Osage, had moved near the Missouri Indian tribe at the Pinnacles in Saline County, Missouri.

There is fair evidence that as early as 1700 the Osage had already changed considerably through their contact with Europeans. The earliest known site where the Osage lived in southwestern Missouri contains much European trade material, and the old culture traits are limited in quantity, but are sufficient to provide insights into their original culture. There is a definite Oneota look about Osage cultural objects, especially the pottery, arrowheads, and pipes. Unfortunately, prehistoric village sites in southwestern Missouri of the people who might have been the progenitors of Osage culture have not been precisely identified. The Osage may have derived from small units, the remains of which have been found primarily in rock shelters and caves. The *Neosho phase* in the four-corners area of Missouri, Kansas, Oklahoma, and Arkansas is possibly the evidence left by the ancestors of the Osage.

Osage pottery is shell tempered and is often decorated with incised and trailed, straight-line hachures. Vessel shapes are primarily jar forms, and some of them have two or more handles or lugs. Perforated pottery disks made from fragments of pottery vessels may have been used as spindle whorls or gaming pieces.

Chipped stonework known to be of Osage derivation consists characteristically of large roughly made scrapers of oval or round form, small flake

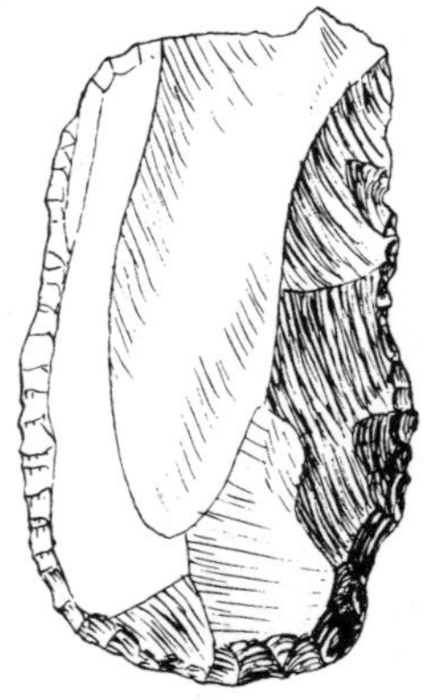

Scraper

Arrowhead

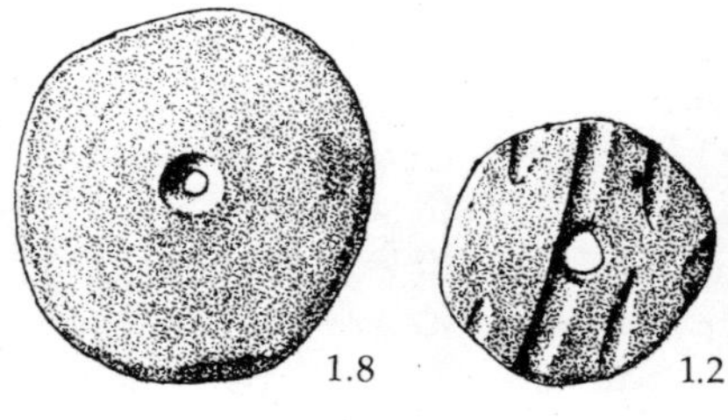

1.8 1.2

Perforated Pottery Disks

end scrapers, small simple triangular arrowheads, and beveled knives. The flaked stone industry was not very important except for the manufacture of arrowheads and scrapers, and the evidence indicates that the craft of flint knapping had degenerated quickly after the fur and hide trade began. Such a decline is to be expected, considering the steady influx, almost from the time of first contact with the Europeans, of Euro-American-made iron scraping and digging tools and guns as weapons. Among the stone tools, the flint scrapers were more satisfactory than the iron, and this superiority probably accounts for the large number of scrapers in proportion to other flint tools found on Osage sites. The bow and arrow continued to be used, but the chipped stone point was soon replaced by brass and iron arrowheads.

Ground-stone items most diagnostic of Osage campsites are metal molds and pipes made of catlinite and other stone. Paired arrowshaft smoothers with a central groove are similar to those made by the Missouri, but not as many are found, perhaps due to their having been made in the approximate proportions as the chipped flint arrowheads. Certainly the two items, arrowshaft smoothers and arrowheads, should complement each other in the industry of producing arrows.

The most common ground-stone tools on the Osage sites are sandstone whetstones of various shapes and sizes. Most of the whetstones are not of any particular size or shape and differ in the abrading property of the stone. A few sharpening stones are of special shapes, truncated cones and narrow ellipses. The latter are similar to the ones found on historic Pawnee

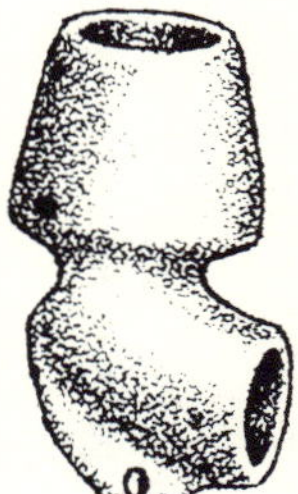

Micmac Pipe

3.9

Catlinite Pipe

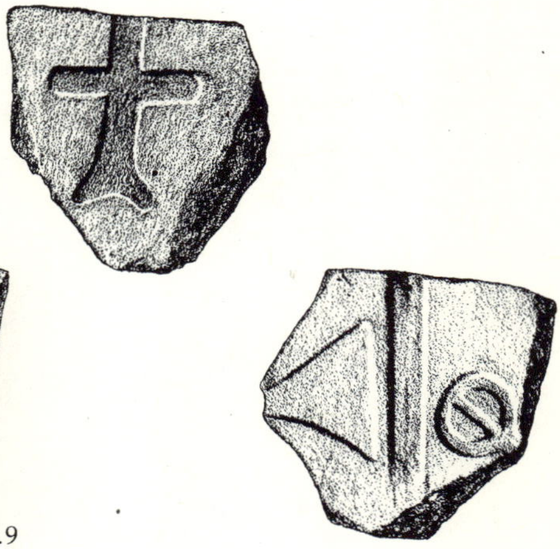

Metal Molds 2.2

sites, and shape as well as use probably derived from European whetstones.

Bone and antler tools consisted of rib arrowshaft straighteners, leg-bone fleshers, mat-weaving needles, bone awls, bone beads, bone buttons, antler flaking tools, and miscellaneous items. Bone handles for iron or steel tools were no doubt European ideas in part, but the use of antler handles for scrapers was an old trait.

Mussel shells are found on the Osage sites, but evidently no tools or ornaments were made of them. The probability is that better items which served the same purpose, such as glass beads, other ornaments, and spoons, could be obtained cheaply and readily from the Euro-American traders.

The archaeological evidences include features such as houses of rectangular ground plan with multiple center posts, straight-sided, teardrop-shaped and bell-shaped pits for storage within the houses, and rectangular trench refuse pits. Small pits approximately a foot in diameter and filled with charred corncobs or wood may have been used for smoking skins. These smudge pits were also within the house structures. Excavations have revealed houses thirty-one to forty-two feet long and fifteen to twenty-two feet wide.

European trade goods make up much of the archaeological remains on Osage sites, and on all but one of the old campsites the trade materials outnumber the native-made items. Brass kettles and articles produced by cutting up and utilizing the brass are prominent in the list of trade goods. Rolled, cylindrical beads, conical tinklers, arrowpoints, and buttons are some of the items made of kettle fragments. Glass beads of various sizes are plentiful, and fragments of glass bottles are present. There is also some crockery, especially on the later sites.

Iron is prevalent on late period Osage campsites; kettle fragments, saws, scissors, files, hoes, and axes make up most of the iron trade goods found. Barrels of trade guns and gun parts take the place of arrowheads, and iron knives replace stone knives. European-made gunflints far outnumber those of Indian manufacture.

Other metal objects such as a few crucifixes, hawk bells, pin brooches, triangular ear-dangles, and tinklers occur in small numbers. The Indians

6

Brass Kettle

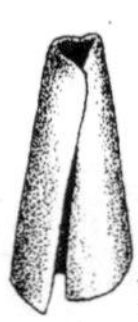

1.4

Tinkler

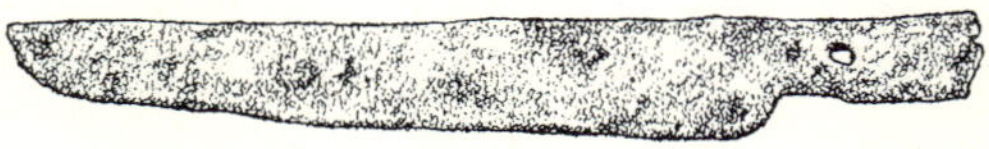

7.5

Iron Knife

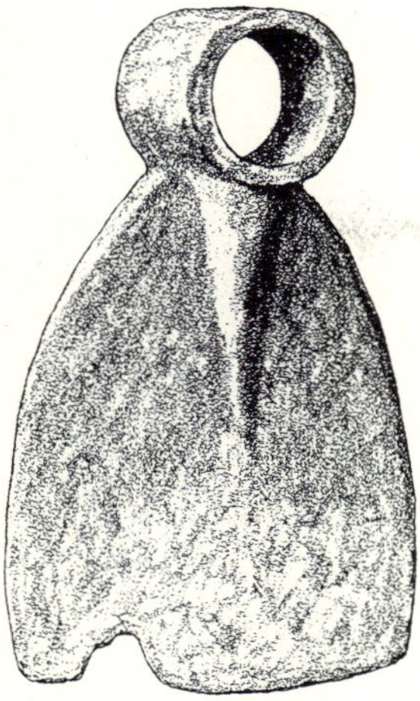

9.4

Iron Hoe

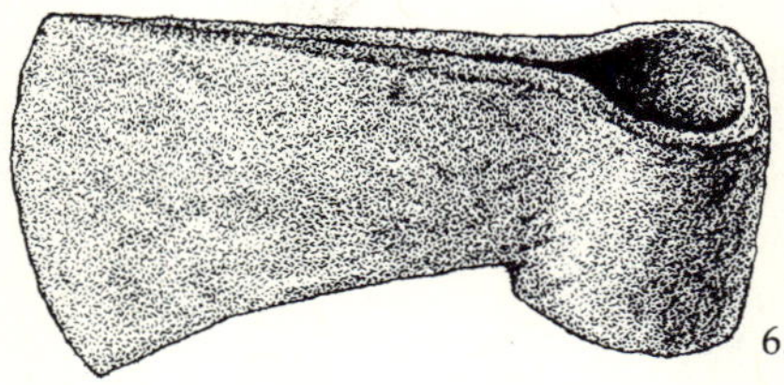

6.3

Iron Ax

themselves occasionally molded decorative items such as crucifixes from lead or pewter in molds which they had carved.

The archaeological picture of the Osage and Missouri is more complete than for any other archaeological groups in a single period. Research is still underway on both, and it is expected that a fuller story of the life of both tribes during the fur and hide trade period will be available in the near future.

Fortunately there are historical sources and ethnographic reports about the lifeways of these aboriginal Missourians. Unfortunately the historical and ethnographical data are from a much later period—a hundred years later than information obtainable from the Osage and Missouri sites in most instances—but it is assumed that general aspects of Osage and Missouri culture such as the ceremonial life and social organization were

1.4

Brass Crucifix

Gun Flints

.4

Hawk Bell

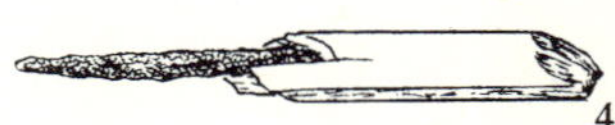

4.5

Iron Awl in Bone Handle

much the same when they lived in Missouri. Although some information is available for the nineteenth century, the most specific information on the nonmaterial aspects of Osage life, their social-political organization and their ceremonial and philosophical beliefs, was not recorded until early in the twentieth century. The Missouri soon lost their cultural identity when they combined with the Oto and Little Osage, and there are no good descriptions of their old culture available.

The following is a selection of the major activities of the Osage compiled from historical and ethnographical sources. The material has been con-

Osage Warrior (after Catlin)

Osage Man (after McKenney and Hall)

densed to give a quick view of the Osage way of life without including the mass of details of the sources from which it was derived.

All people must eat, sleep, and perform the natural functions associated with biological group living. The way these functions and actions are performed and the tools and devices for their performance, whether actual, fictional, material, social, ceremonial, or religious, make it possible to separate groups of people and to recognize them as distinct units such as Osage Indians or Missouri Indians. The following description is a synopsis of Osage culture, the unique, recognizable Osage way of life.

The Osage were at home in a village situated on an eminence, a high terrace, or a high prairie which overlooked lower ground and which usually had some moundlike hill in sight. At the time the French first encountered the Osage, villages may have been an organized camp circle with each clan assuming its proper place according to rank and function in both political and ceremonial endeavors. The chief's house, somewhat larger in size, may have been inside the circle. Houses were rectangular in ground plan, at least fifteen feet wide and varying from thirty to forty-seven or more feet in length. Center posts crotched at the top were spaced about eight to twelve feet apart and supported a ridgepole. Over it were bent poles that formed the roof. They were attached to wall posts at least five feet in height and spaced a few inches to two feet apart. There were crossbars at right angles to the upright wall posts, and the bent roof stringers attached to them. The arborlike framework was covered with overlapping woven rush mats about three feet wide and four feet long. The weaving tool was a long flat needle made of a buffalo rib.

The doorways were on the long side of the house, and when houses were in proper ceremonial order, one doorway opened to the east. One or more fireplaces—shallow, scooped-out areas about one and one-half to two feet in diameter—were located near the longitudinal center line of the houses and spaced ten to twelve feet apart, with smoke holes in the roof above each fireplace. In some of the houses there were storage pits, placed toward the center but away from the fireplaces. The pits may have been a means of protecting skin clothing as well as food from the dogs, which were never fed, but lived by preying and on what they could steal.

Small smudge pits in the floor near the walls were used for curing skins. The scraped hides were stretched on a framework over a slow-burning corncob fire, and the smoking toughened the hides for use in making moccasins or skin boats.

A low bench about three feet high, sometimes placed at one end of the house, was used for the storage of valuables, including such things as animal skins. In the chief's house this bench was assigned to honored guests for their convenience while visiting the chief. The furniture in all houses consisted of woven rush mats, which were spread for sitting or sleeping near the fireplace.

Movable household items other than the mats in early times—until 1725 to 1750—consisted of pottery cooking vessels kept near the fireplaces. Later they were replaced by brass and iron kettles. A wooden bowl was the individual's personal dish. Food was served with spoons, but the fingers and a knife were used in eating. The earliest spoons were probably made of shell and the later ones of horn. Gourds may have been used as water containers. Guests were offered food in wooden bowls until the introduction of copper kettles, which tended to replace the bowls.

Fire was kindled by means of a simple firestick rubbed rapidly back and forth between the palms, the end of the stick resting in a small hollow in a dry piece of wood. With the introduction of flint and steel for firemaking, the slower friction method was dropped. Fire tongs—split sticks with which live coals could be handled—were kept near the fireplaces, as were small brooms made by tying together bundles of reeds or rushes.

A quiver of arrows and a bow made of bois d'arc (Osage orange) hung from the center post, on the side walls, or on the bench at the end of the house. A flintlock trade gun, accompanied by a powder horn, might replace the bow and arrow or be an addition to them.

The cradleboard was an item of furniture in every Osage household. It was basically a board three feet long and about one foot wide and square at the ends. It usually had a frame that protruded a foot or more in front of the place where the child's head would lie. The occipital flattening of the child's head that resulted from resting against the hard back of the cradleboard was considered attractive by the Osage. Children were desirable, and in a large household there would normally be at least one of the age to be strapped in a cradleboard.

Items of clothing, especially finery for ceremonies, were hung from the rafters or walls out of reach of the voracious dogs that occasionally dodged into the house or dug under the walls. Skins in the process of being made into clothing might be hung from the ceiling or hidden in storage pits. Skin bags of dried meat, strings of water-lily roots, and prepared persimmon cakes were suspended from the rafters, and it is logical that the woven mats of dried pumpkin were stored in the same manner. Thus the inside walls and ceiling of an Osage house would display many items of interest.

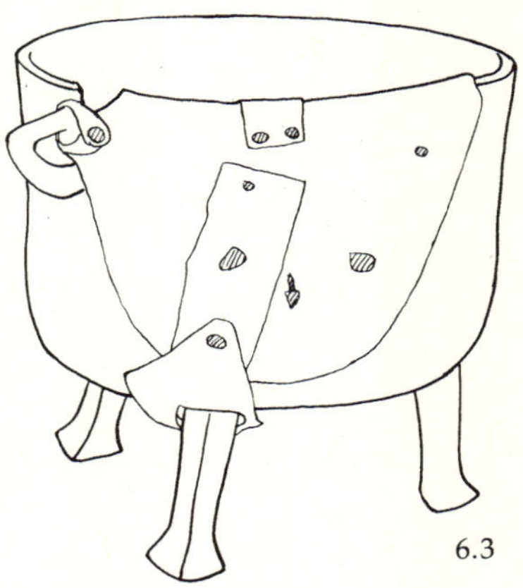

6.3

Mended Iron Kettle

Moving outside the house during the daytime, when no ceremonies were in progress, one would have noted various activities. Several women might be preparing skins for clothing or bedding. One of the processes in skin preparation for certain purposes was the removal of the hair, using a hafted scraper of adzlike form, and another was the softening of the skin by pulling it from side to side through a small loop of sinew attached to a stout post.

Weaving rush mats was a major activity. When the rushes had been collected and properly dried, mats were woven, partly twilled and partly plain weave. Belts, garters, and ornaments of buffalo hair were woven or plaited on a belt loom.

Racks for drying meat, pumpkins, lily roots, and corn were near the house so they could be guarded from prowling animals. Slow-burning, small fires may have been a means of speeding up the process of smoking or drying these foods.

During many months of the year the permanent village was abandoned by all but a few old men and women and some children. The people able to do so went on hunting and gathering excursions at times best suited to obtain the game or product. The villages of those on the move were different in that the houses were smaller and often took the form of the dome-shaped wigwam so characteristic of the northeastern United States. Another difference was that some of the cooking fires were outside the house structure, and more activity took place in the open air. The major business in the temporary camp was the preparation of the particular item sought by the hunting or collecting party.

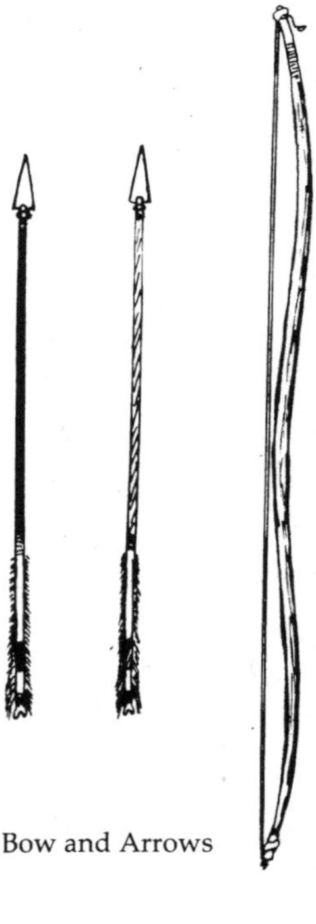

Bow and Arrows

The hunting cycle was approximately as follows. The first hunt of the year, or spring hunt, was for bear, and when the fur trade with Europeans became important, the bear hunt was followed by a beaver hunt. The members of the hunting party returned to the permanent village in time for the women to plant the gardens in April. The summer hunt for buffalo or deer usually began in May and lasted until time to harvest the garden crops. The fall hunt for buffalo or deer sometimes began as early as September and lasted until December, but much of October and part of November was spent in gathering persimmons and nuts.

The regular hunts were highly organized, and most of the village participated in them in spite of the fact that the men alone did the hunting. The women butchered, dried, and smoked the meat and prepared the skins for transport back to the permanent village.

Theoretically, there were two tribal chiefs, one from each moiety or dual social-political division of the tribe, who took turns each day in conducting the journey both to and from the camp. The chiefs selected and appointed soldiers of the hunt. The soldiers kept order during the hunting trip and made certain that all had an equal chance at the game. There were four captains and a leader of hunt soldiers. The captains saw to it that any soldiers who failed to do their duty were punished, and one of the captains acted as a town crier. In practice, a single temporary chief was often selected in council to lead the hunting party. He was responsible for the hunt and shared in the rewards if the hunt were successful or helped bear the losses if it were unsuccessful.

Hunting was serious business, but the trips were always joyous times when the hunting was good. There was plenty of food, and everyone was busy. Excitement prevailed; almost each day young men earned honors, and all gained new food and raw materials for clothing and utensils. Perhaps part of the thrill of the hunt was the excursion into new territory or the return to old haunts visited only occasionally—the remembrance of accomplishments at particular places and the recollection of events that transpired there—all adding to the excitement and pleasure.

The men hunted the game, and the women and children gathered the edible plant foods. Persimmons, nuts, and water-lily roots were the items most sought after. Persimmons were seeded and made into cakes. The cakes, two to four layers thick, were baked on boards which were about nine inches wide and eighteen inches long and had a handle so that they could be held over the coals.

The American lotus, a large water lily, the seeds and roots of which were important food, was considered sacred and had a place in the tribal rites. The roots were gathered with ceremony similar to that of the Missouri. The lotus roots were scraped and cut into one- or two-inch sections, strung on a thong, and hung on racks to dry. The seeds were eaten raw or were roasted.

Gardening was an integral part of the Osage way of life. The women planted, watched, and harvested the crops. In April they sowed the seeds along the watercourses in areas free of grass and trees. Old vegetation was raked away, and hills for the seed were made with hoes. The gardener first

10.5

Bone Mat-Weaving Needle

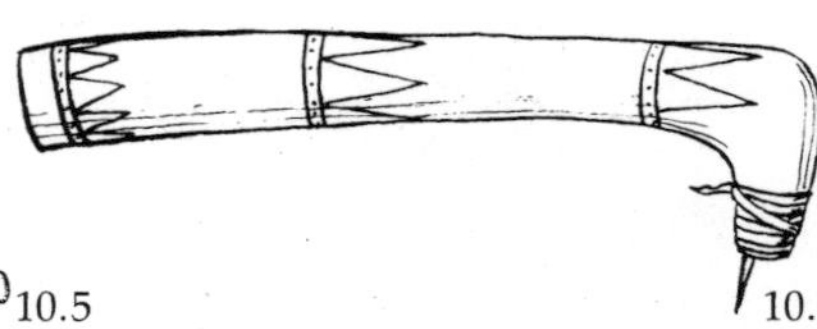
10.5

Hafted Scraper

punched a hole with a digging stick—a straight, pointed stick—dropped in the seeds, and closed the hole by stepping on it. The gardens, which at most were one-half acre per family, were laid out in adjoining fields, unfenced. The crops were cultivatd only once, using hoes. This was in May, just before the summer hunt, and the gardeners usually went on the hunt, leaving the few villagers who stayed at home to look after the garden in a general way from May through July.

Corn, beans, and squash were the crops grown; yields were from thirty to sixty bushels per acre of corn and beans together. August was harvest time. Most of the corn was picked in the roasting-ear stage with the husk on so that several ears could be braided together by the inner husks and hung to dry in the houses. Boiling and roasting the corn on the cob were the prevalent cooking methods either for immediate use or for preservation. The corn was dried after it had been cooked. When dry it was removed from the cob and pounded into a fine meal in a wooden mortar or between two stones. As this cornmeal was already cooked, it needed only water to expand it—an early example of instant mix. It could also be eaten dry and thus became a light-weight concentrated food that could be carried on hunting or war parties, capable of sustaining the food needs of an individual for several days. Parched corn and hominy made from corn that was picked after it had matured and dried were other dishes prepared by the Osage.

Squash and pumpkin were preserved by peeling the skins from the pulp, removing the seeds, and cutting the pulp into long strips which were hung in the sun to dry. When the strips were partly dehydrated they were braided or woven into oblong mats. These were hung over racks and were smoked or heated to aid the preservation.

Women played an extremely important part in Osage life in spite of the fact that their work was greatly undervalued by the men. Each morning—to meet the day bravely—the girls had the part in their hair painted red to represent long life, the path of the sun as it travels across the sky. The work of food preparation, cooking, and preservation was done by the women. Also the gardening and gathering were primarily the jobs of the girls and women. Women manufactured most of the essential items of the home and constructed the house itself. They prepared the animal skins obtained on the hunt and fabricated from them items of clothing and useful household utensils.

Among the Osage, as among most people, the family was the important kinship unit, and an individual's prestige and position in the society were dependent first upon his or her family and the social obligations expected of it. Marriage was an important function regulated not only by the family but also by the clan for its greatest advantage. Clans were composed of

people related by blood and some adopted members that might even be of different tribes. Clans were patrilineal, exogamous social units that were the basic, integral parts of the political, social, and ceremonial organization of the tribe.

The moiety was a political organization that cut across family and clan lines and held extra significance above them. The Osage village was divided into two moieties—the Peace or Household and the War or Sacred One. They were made up of five phratries, each phratry being a series of clan and sub-clan groupings. The moieties had a variety of duties such as the initiation of new members into the secret society, and participation in war and hunting ceremonies. Members of one moiety had to choose their mates from the other moiety, indicating that regulation of marriage may have been their major function. Healing may have been another moiety activity. Although each moiety had a chief, the one taking precedence was associated with the Peace or Household moiety.

Chieftainship was an inherited position within particular families. Usually the son of the deceased chief was chosen, but it was necessary for him to be qualified for the position. The selection could be made from any of the sons, nephews, uncles, or other family members; it was not primogeniture alone that determined the choice of a chief.

The power of the chief was limited. He was the leader of the council rather than the ruler, in regard to decisions concerning civil functions. The true governing body seems to have been the assembly of "Little Old Men," a council of men who had taken the seven degrees in the secret or religious society of the tribe.

Other important officials were the marmitons—town criers, grand chamberlains, and principal cooks for the chiefs. They were highly respected personages and often were warriors who had lost their families, had been injured, or were too old to carry arms.

The social, political, and ceremonial organizations were interrelated, and the religious and philosophical beliefs of the Osage appear to have been closely integrated with social-political-ceremonial organization. This close relationship found expression in a secret religious society. Each clan and moiety had specific functions in regard to the ceremonies of the religious society, and each clan had a life symbol and a mythology as an inherent right.

In order for an Osage man to reach a prominent position he had to be initiated into the seven degrees of the religious order. The council of the Little Old Men was made up of those who had been so initiated and instructed by their predecessors. They comprised the religious as well as the socio-political leaders and conducted the major rites.

War ceremonies were very important and were the means by which the male members of the society could gain prestige. The mourning ceremony was especially significant. Mourning and war were the only situations in which violence was accepted as normal, and this acceptance was in effect a means of directing strongly emotional expressions into warfare and the accompanying rituals.

In 1806 the Osage were living in three villages, two in Vernon County, Missouri, and one near Claremore, Oklahoma. In 1808 they gave up all their rights to lands in Missouri east of a line drawn from Fort Osage due south. This line lay east of their villages at the time. In 1823 they moved west to Kansas and Oklahoma, and in 1825, again by treaty with the United States, they ceded all the rest of their lands in Missouri to the United States.

Suggested Reading

Bailey, Garrick A., 1973. *Changes in Osage Social Organization 1673–1906.* University of Oregon Press, Eugene.

Bray, Robert T., 1961. "The Missouri Indian Tribe in Archaeology and History." *Missouri Historical Review* 45(3): 213–25.

Chapman, Carl H., 1959. "The Little Osage and Missouri Indian Village Sites, ca. 1727–1777." *The Missouri Archaeologist* 21(1): 1–67.

Chapman, Carl H., 1974a. *Osage Indians III: The Origin of the Osage Indian Tribe.* Garland Publishing, Inc., New York.

Chapman, Carl H., 1974b. "The Indomitable Osage in the Spanish Illinois (Upper Louisiana), 1763–1804." In *The Spanish in the Mississippi Valley 1762–1804,* edited by John F. McDermott, pp. 287–313, University of Illinois Press, Urbana.

Chapman, Carl H., 1982. "Osage Indians in Missouri and Oklahoma, A.D. 1796–1825." In *Pathways to Plains Prehistory,* edited by Don G. Wyckoff and Jack L. Hofman. Oklahoma Anthropological Society Memoir, 3: 19–28.

Spider Life Symbol

Hamilton, T. M., compiler, 1960. "Indian Trade Guns." *The Missouri Archaeologist* 22 (whole volume).

Hamilton, T. M., 1980. *Colonial Frontier Guns.* The Fur Press, Chadron, Nebraska.

Horr, David A., ed., 1974. *Osage Indians I, II, IV, and V.* Garland Publishing, Inc., New York.

La Flesche, Francis, 1921. *The Osage Tribe.* Smithsonian Institution, Bureau of American Ethnology, Annual Report 36, U.S. Government Printing Office, Washington, D.C.

La Flesche, Francis, 1932. *Dictionary of the Osage Language.* Smithsonian Institution, Bureau of American Ethnology, Bulletin 109, U.S. Government Printing Office, Washington, D.C.

McDermott, John F., 1940. *Tixier's Travels on the Osage Prairies.* University of Oklahoma Press, Norman.

Matthews, John J., 1961. *The Osages: Children of the Middle Waters.* University of Oklahoma Press, Norman.

7.5

Inlaid Catlinite Pipe

10.5

War Bundle Pipe and Stem

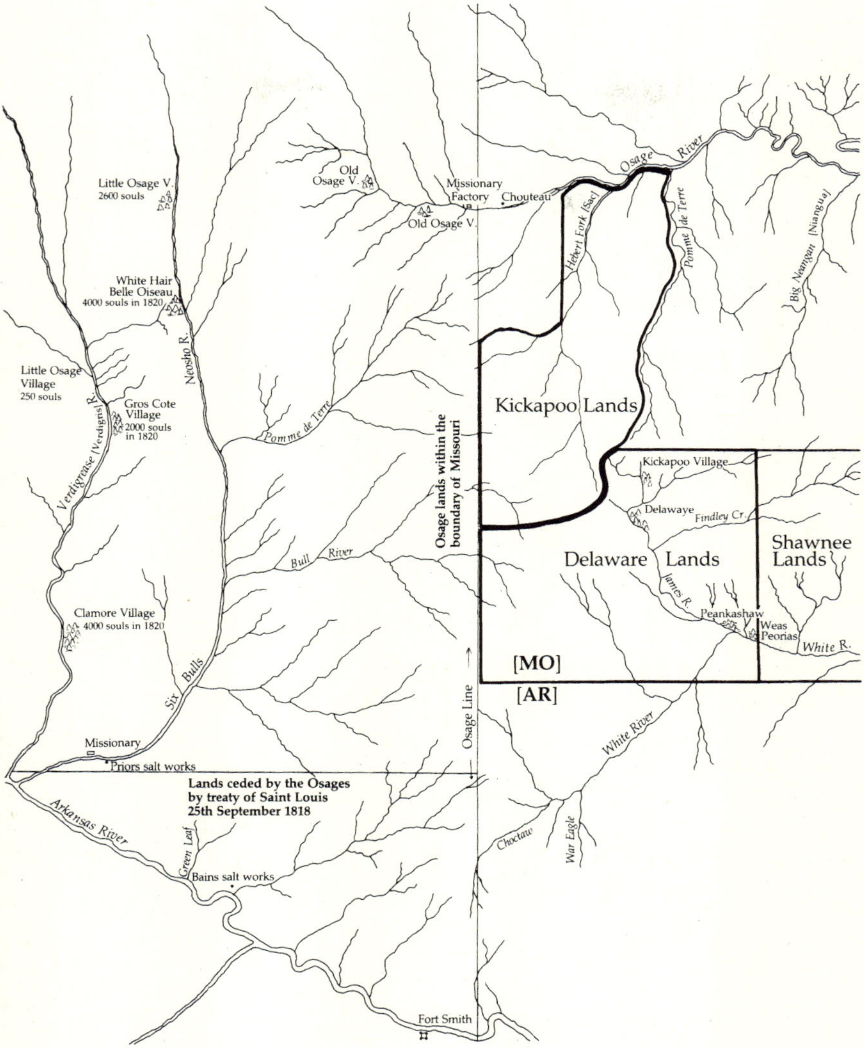

Composite Map Showing Indian Lands and Villages about 1820

The Remnants: Tribes Passing through Missouri

The native tribes of Missouri held their territory in the central and western part of the state until the first quarter of the nineteenth century. In spite of the fact that the Osage gave up all claims to land in the central and eastern part of the state by the treaty of 1808, they continued to use much of the area described in the treaty until Missouri became a state. The Missouri tribe had left before 1800, and by 1808 the Osage permanent villages were all west of the Osage Line drawn due south from Fort Osage (Sibley, Missouri).

The Delaware and Shawnee had moved into Missouri from the northeast at the invitation of the Spanish governors of Louisiana in 1789 to serve as a deterrent and buffer between the Spanish colonies and the hostile Osage Indians. They settled on Apple and Shawnee creeks between Cape Girardeau and St. Louis, at a safe distance from the Osage permanent villages, approximately two hundred miles away. In the 1790s the Delaware and Shawnee were two of several tribes making raids on the Osage at the instigation of the Spanish who, until 1794, intended to destroy the Osage. The Delaware and Shawnee were the first of the transient Indians to have absolute claims on lands in what is now Missouri. One band or village of the Shawnee moved to the mouth of the Bourbeuse River and maintained a town there for several years. There is evidence that the Shawnee helped supply St. Louis with meat at least until the War of 1812 and continued to live in villages west of St. Louis. Some of them were on Huzzah Creek in Crawford County in 1818.

During the War of 1812 there were many movements of the Indian tribes that took part in the conflict either for or against the British. Among them were the Kickapoo, who were given a reservation on the Pomme de Terre and Osage rivers in Benton, Hickory, and Greene counties in 1819. The Pomme de Terre River formed the eastern boundary of the reservation, and a major village was located where the city of Springfield is now.

During the same period, the Delaware were located on a reservation to the south of the Kickapoo and established a village on the James Fork of White River. The Shawnee held land east of the Delaware reservation. The Delaware and Shawnee and the Kickapoo retained their reservations until 1829 and 1832, respectively.

The Iowa tribe hunted in northern Missouri, especially in the upper reaches of north Grand River, which has its headwaters in Iowa. They may have had villages in the northern part of Missouri, but if so, their locations have yet to be found. One site at King Hill, St. Joseph, Missouri, may be an Iowa site, but is likely Kansas Indian. The Kansas Indians were closely

Delaware Chief (after Hesselius)

Iowa Warrior (after McKenney and Hall)

related culturally to the Osage and were classed together linguistically as Dhegiha Sioux.

There is no doubt that the Illinois tribes had villages in Missouri for short periods. Some of the early maps place a village of the Cahokia tribe several miles below St. Louis on the west side of the Mississippi, and the Kaskaskia were living in what is now south St. Louis when the "Mound City" was still young.

4.5

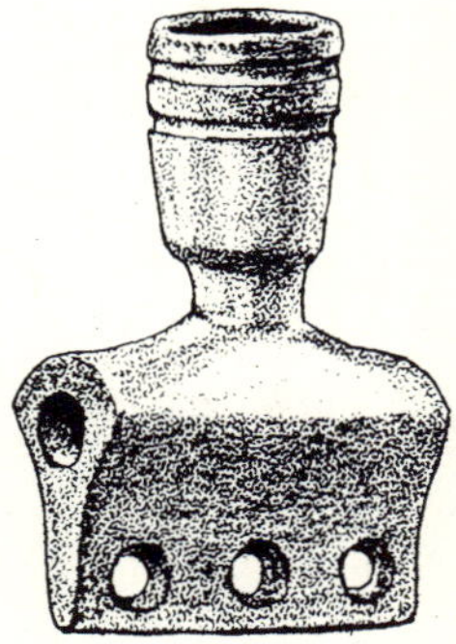

2.8

Catlinite Pipes

In southwestern Missouri a number of tribes were present for a short time and were recorded by some of the map makers. They were the Piankashaw, the Peoria, and the Wea. The Cherokee may have hunted in southern Missouri, but Cherokee lands were south and west in Arkansas and Oklahoma.

In the northeastern part of the state the Sauk (Sac) and Fox hunted, subsequent to the War of 1812. Before and after that time they occasionally made raids against the Missouri or the Osage. The Sauk and Fox were important in the history of Missouri following her elevation to statehood, and there were numerous encounters between these tribes and the settlers in northeastern Missouri. The Sauk and Fox claimed much of northeastern Missouri.

None of the transient tribes remained long enough in any one place in Missouri to leave sufficient archaeological evidences to identify their locations so far as is known. Furthermore, historic accounts which describe the tribes passing through Missouri fail to tell much about the Indians and their customs. Most of the Indians at this time were from the east and had had contacts with the European way of life for at least two hundred years before they came to Missouri. Many European customs had been adopted by them, and the casual observer living in the area seldom found the Indians' dress or habits strikingly different enough to record. These remnants of once powerful tribes in the east were relatively few in number and did not remain long in Missouri. Except for catlinite pipes and trade goods, they left very few marks of their passing through the state.

Suggested Reading

Baird, David W., 1980. *The Quapaw Indians: A History of the Downstream People.* University of Oklahoma Press, Norman.

Foreman, Grant, 1936. *Indians and Pioneers.* University of Oklahoma Press, Norman.

Foreman, Grant, 1946. *The Last Trek of the Indians.* University of Chicago Press, Chicago.

Foreman, Grant, 1953 (new ed.). *Indian Removal.* University of Oklahoma Press, Norman.

Gibson, A. M., 1963. *The Kickapoos.* University of Oklahoma Press, Norman.

McDermott, John F., 1955. *Indian Sketches.* University of Oklahoma Press, Norman.

Nasatir, Abraham P., 1952. *Before Lewis and Clark.* 2 vols., St. Louis Historical Documents Foundation, St. Louis.

Newcomb, William W., Jr., 1956. *The Culture and Acculturation of the Delaware Indians.* Anthropological Papers, Museum of Anthropology, University of Michigan, no. 10, Ann Arbor.

Unrau, William E., 1979. *The Emigrant Indians of Kansas: A Critical Bibliography.* Indiana University Press, Bloomington.

Weslager, C. A., 1972. *The Delaware Indians: A History.* Rutgers University Press, New Brunswick, New Jersey.

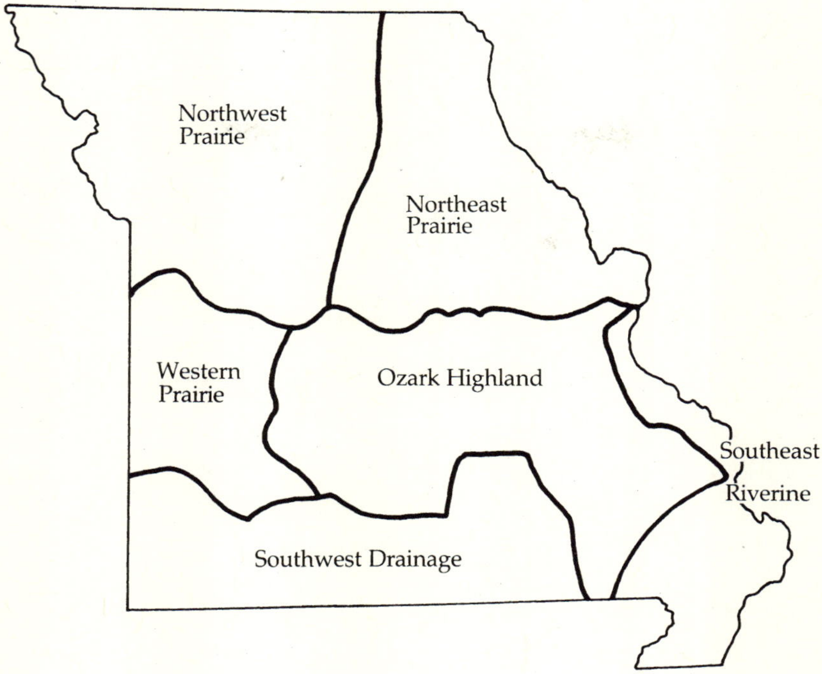

Archaeological Regions

Period	Time	Tradition	Representative and Diagnostic Cultural Materials
Middle Woodland	500 B.C.	Prairie Forest Potter	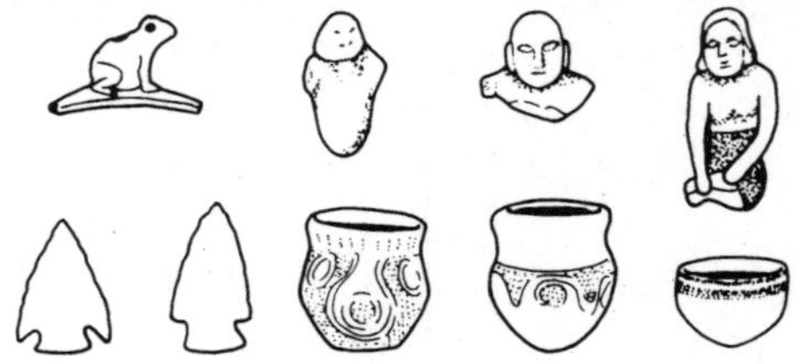
Early Woodland	1000 B.C.	Prairie Forest Potter	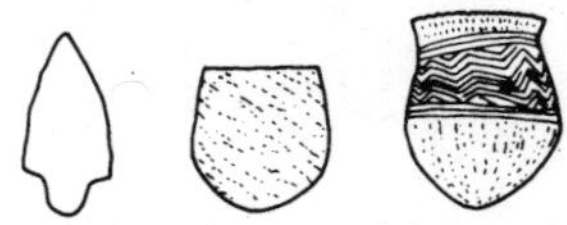
Late Archaic	3000 B.C.	Forager	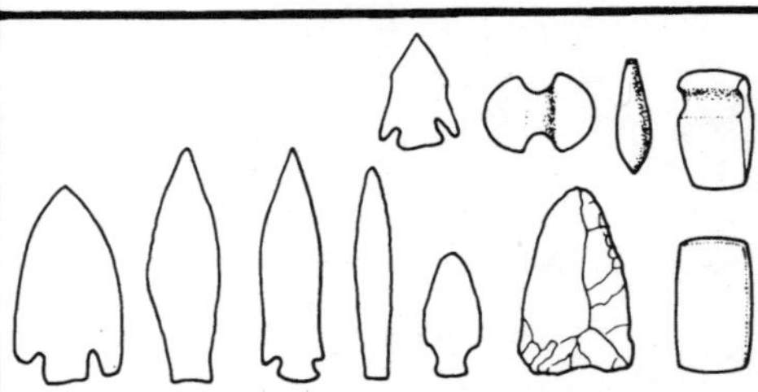
Middle Archaic	5000 B.C.	Forager	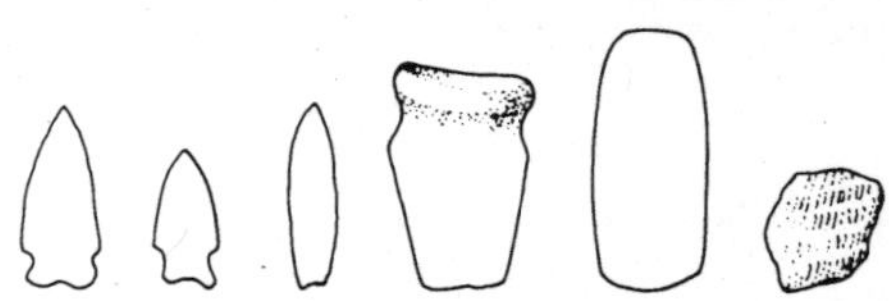
Early Archaic	7000 B.C.	Forager	
Dalton	8000 B.C.	Hunter-Forager	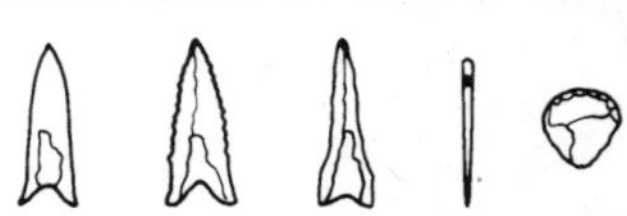
Paleo-Indian	12,000 B.C.	Early Hunter	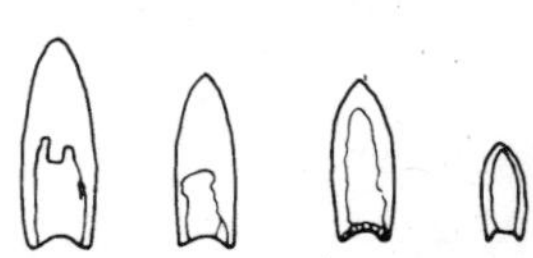

Period	Time	Tradition	Representative and Diagnostic Cultural Materials
Historic	A.D. 1673	Known Indian Tribes	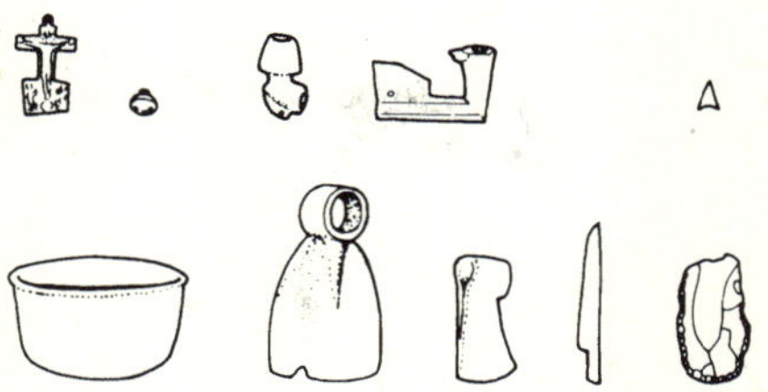
Proto-Historic	A.D. 1450	Oneota and Village Farmer	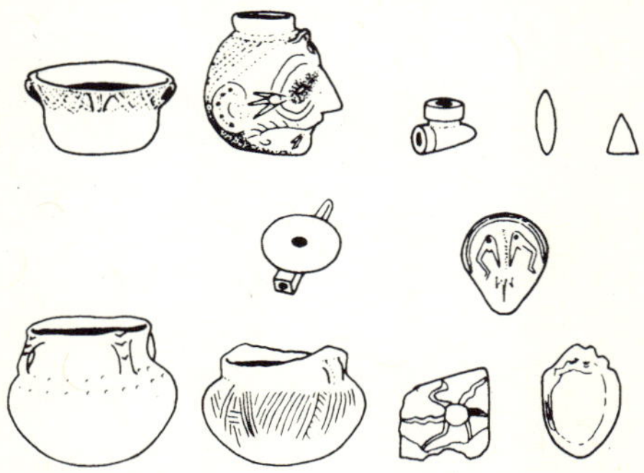
Mississippi	A.D. 900	Village Farmer	
Late Woodland	A.D. 400	Prairie Forest Potter	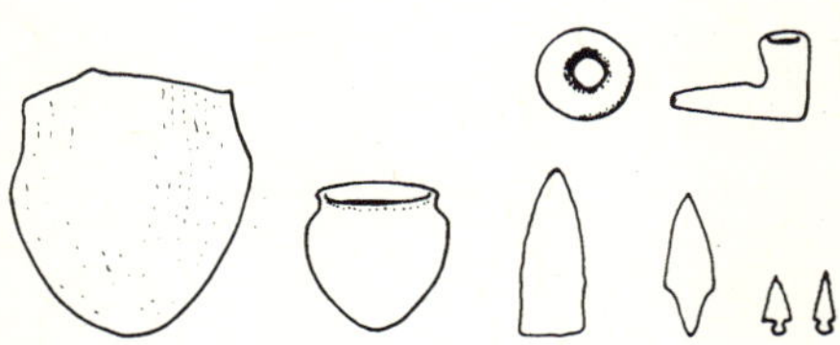

The Archaeological Survey of Missouri

Some day when you are driving down a back road near a stream, your curiosity may be aroused by the sight of several people walking across a cultivated field. They will stoop frequently, pick up something, and place it in a paper bag that each is carrying. They will seem oblivious to the surroundings, keeping their gaze to the ground as they search the fields systematically. If you should stop and inquire about their unusual actions, you might stay and join them, for they are enthusiastic people having fun looking into the past. These men and women are part of more than a thousand in the state who have archaeology as their avocation or vocation, and they are searching for the remains of the earliest Missourians.

Fifty years ago, little was known about Missouri's past prior to A.D. 1673. It was known that the Indians had lived here before the French rediscovered the state, but it was only suspected that they had lived here for thousands of years. During the last half century through the efforts of hundreds of people who have been interested in the prehistory of Missouri, solid evidence has been found that the state has been continuously occupied by Indians for more than twelve thousand years. Our written

history, beginning with the voyage down the Mississippi River in 1673 by Marquette and Jolliet, is a short time by comparison.

One of the most frequently asked questions is, "How do you know where to look for Indian sites and artifacts?" The usual answer is, "Look first for a good supply of water, as the Indians had to have water close at hand." It is estimated that 80 percent or more of the Indian campsites and town sites are located in river valleys or adjacent to springs or other fresh-water sources. Looking for a water supply is not the only answer, because water courses have changed over the thousands of years that the Indians have lived in Missouri, the water table has lowered, and there were features besides water that caused the Indians to select particular places for their campsites and other activities.

Another question asked almost as frequently is, "What do you look for?" The answer to this is more involved, but the things searched for are generally the trash which accumulated at camp and village sites. This trash consists of broken implements; utensils of stone, bone, shell, and pottery; and flint chips and spalls that are the wastage from the manufacture of chipped stone tools. These evidences are hunted in the open fields and terraces, along the river banks, and near the mouths of caves or under overhanging ledges forming shelters that might have been used by the Indians. Mounds and other earthworks are also looked for along the bluffs

as well as in the stream valleys, but they are not always easily identified as man-made, as there are many natural mounds in the state of Missouri.

"How do you make a survey for archaeological sites?" The first step is to obtain the best available map of the area that is planned to be surveyed. Surveying without a map is like shaving without a blade in your razor. A United States Geological Survey topographic quadrangle map, if available for the particular place where the survey is planned, may be the best. Such a map shows streams, roads, houses, churches, places of special interest, towns, and differences in elevation, all useful in locating a particular place on the map. Sometimes the topographic quadrangle maps are old and the new roads are not shown, in which case it is advisable to obtain the latest county highway map and use it in conjunction with the quadrangle map for making the survey. Quadrangle maps are available at the office of the State Geologist, Missouri Geological Survey and Water Resources Division, Department of Natural Resources, Rolla, Missouri, and county highway maps may be obtained from the State Highway Department, Jefferson City, Missouri.

Once the decision has been made as to the area to be surveyed, the first place to check on the map is the house nearest the starting point of the survey. Go to the house and find out who owns the property to be surveyed. Permission must be obtained from the owner, for it is trespassing to go through the property without permission. Furthermore, the owner will probably be able to help you by pointing out where evidences such as arrowheads or flint chippings, mounds, or other remains have been seen. In many instances the landowner has picked up some of the things, and they are of historical interest and should be recorded. Always remember that no one has the right to go on another's land without permission. Respect the owner's rights, close gates, stay out of muddy fields in which there are crops, and avoid any destruction of property. Furthermore, don't carry a gun; you are searching for historical evidences, not game!

The most likely places to look are in stream valleys on well-drained terraces that have been plowed and rained upon. A zigzag course across a terrace will very quickly turn up evidence of a campsite if one is there. If indications are found, make a sketch map of the site and divide it into equal units depending upon the quantity of materials. For example, six-meter or twenty-foot squares are usually sufficient for most sites. Number the squares on your sketch map and place the site number and the unit number on a bag before you pick up any items noted. Then if there are numerous items in a square, note on a sketch map of the square the position of each item in it and give each a separate number or letter. Write it on the artifact with a soft lead pencil or put each in a separate small container with the number on it before placing it in the square bag.

The Indian's home was a workshop, and the by-products of tool manufacture and items broken in manufacture are commonly found on a camp location. Fragments of pottery vessels are the most common evidences in the lowland of southeastern Missouri where stone is relatively scarce. Unfinished tools and broken implements such as arrowheads, knives,scrapers, adzes, and axes are common, for many tools were broken while being made or used and were discarded. Complete specimens are also found, although less frequently, for they were generally lost or misplaced rather than thrown away and are relatively few in comparison to those that were broken in manufacture or use. The broken artifacts should be collected, for they are often just as important as the complete tools in working out the history of the site. It is almost impossible to obtain a representative sample of the location from whole artifacts, and it is equally difficult to get a good sample without including the broken artifacts. The best thing to do is to map in all surface materials, record their locations as accurately as possible, and then place them in a bag that has been marked before taking them home and washing them. They should then be recorded in a ledger or notebook. Once recorded so that the artifact can be found readily on your sketch map, a number should be assigned to it and placed on the item as well as in the ledger or notebook. All broken artifacts, flakes, cores, potsherds, bones, and any other things possibly useful for the interpretation should be recorded. When marked by site location and place in the area (three- to six-meter or ten- to twenty-foot squares), they are useful in working out settlement patterns and the lifeway activities of the prehistoric people. It would be best if each item were marked individually or kept in separate, marked bags or boxes until they are studied by archaeologists interested in using them for the interpretation of the prehistory of the area. Better yet, try making the interpretation yourself. Read about the techniques for identifying certain activity areas such as preparation of food, cooking it, and disposing of the trash associated with it. These in turn normally take place in a house or shelter of some kind, so identifying the activity area may also provide the location of the structure in which the activity took place. The relationship of the activity areas or house locations or the pattern they form can in turn be used to estimate the population size and internal arrangement of the campsite or village. The relative size of the house areas and the quality of the artifacts associated with each may evidence a differentiation in status of the individuals that lived there, and so on. By observing and recording in detail everything on a site you can forge ahead with interpretations yourself. Frequent visits, after each cultivation for example, should aid in learning about what is underground without ever turning a spadeful of dirt.

One easy way to locate activity areas is to use surveyors' flags to mark all of the artifacts, leaving the flags and artifacts in place until a fair part of the field has been traversed. This procedure makes it possible to see what area has been covered and to determine the clusters of materials denoting activity areas. It also makes it easier to record each item accurately on your map.

Items such as burned rock, pottery sherds, burned clay, charcoal, and split bones if found in a small area probably denote a hearth and the cooking of food. The hearth is probably in a house structure. Sometimes the location of houses on a site can be ascertained by the concentration or clustering of flags at intervals in the field when the flagging technique is used. In such cases you can almost literally see the organization of the houses on the campsite by the clusters of flags, particularly if you have focused on marking the evidences of fireplaces or hearths. Visualizing the campsite as it may have been when the Indian lived there in this manner and reconstructing it on paper, on your map, is even more exciting than finding a perfect arrowhead, and eventually you can become an expert on that site, and for that matter on a local area if you cover a number of sites in your locality.

Sometimes after a campsite is located, there is the problem of finding its limits or the area that should be mapped. Soil color may be helpful because the addition of humus through camp refuse darkens the soil. In some instances camp debris is scattered continuously over a river terrace or hilltop without easily discernible areas of concentration. The probable reason for such extensive distribution of evidences is the use of separate parts of the site for camping at different times by distinct groups of people.

In this case the various camp locations must be isolated by the concentrations of materials distinctive of the different groups; for example, the distribution of a particular pottery type in the field could indicate the location of one of the camps, and the locations of flint flakes and chipped flint artifacts that have not been heat treated might denote another. Sometimes if there have been many different occupations on the site for a long time period and if also the field has been cultivated for a hundred years or more, it may be nearly impossible to determine the separate site limits or to locate the activity areas. Even in this instance it is desirable to locate all the artifacts accurately, for eventually your compilation may allow for separation of one or more of the components, or separate occupations of the site.

It is important to record the size of the campsite if at all possible. On many sites it is fairly easy to determine limits of the evidences which thin

Temple Mound

Burial Mound

Rock Cairn

Rock Structure and Burials inside Mound

out and then disappear. Such sites can be measured simply by pacing or stepping off the length and width of the area covered by evidences. A usual pace is two and one half to three feet in length, and a great pace or two steps is five to six feet. For many people walking their normal gait, the use of a pace is probably accurate enough. It is easy to determine one's pace by measuring off one hundred or two hundred feet, walking the distance normally, and then dividing the number of steps into the distance that was measured. It would be advisable to measure two hundred feet in a straight line and to walk the distance several times in order to obtain an average pace.

The size of the campsite is important; it has been found as a general rule that the earlier the site the smaller it is. The size of campsites tends to increase toward the historic period.

Caves and overhanging rock ledges were used as campsites by certain Indians. The places normally selected were large, dry, and well lighted. Caves generally were lived in only as far as the light from the entrance penetrated. Evidences of the use of natural shelters can be found near the opening, where water dripping from the ledges above has washed out broken tools, flint chips, and pottery sherds. The same types of material will be evident inside the cave or shelter where burrowing animals have dug them up.

Uncovering Rock-Lined Cists

In recording shelter sites, the depth of the shelter or the distance from the overhang to the back wall should be given. The height of the ledge or roof from the floor and the distance the overhang covers along the bluff are also needed. Cave measurements should include width and height of entrance and the distance to which the light penetrates. These dimensions as well as any evidence concerning the depth and type of deposit that covers the floor of the cave or shelter are important to the archaeologist.

Mounds and other earthworks of large size are fairly characteristic structures in the lowland areas in southeastern Missouri. Many of the mounds are a truncated pyramid in shape and were used as the base for a chief's house or a ceremonial structure. Such mounds are large and prominent. Groups of mounds are sometimes bordered by ditches and embankments. The embankments had large wooden palisades on top of them to protect the village from attack. Similar types of structures on hilltops in central Missouri, such as the "Old Fort" at Van Meter State Park, are thought to have been ceremonial rather than defensive. Small rounded mounds associated with the large fortified mound sites usually were house locations.

Many of the small hemispherical mounds are burial mounds. In the highland or Ozark uplift area and along the Missouri River and its tributar-

Petroglyphs at Washington State Park

ies, burial mounds are generally found on the summits of bluffs. They vary in size from fifteen to one hundred feet in diameter. Their interiors often contain rock structures housing human bones. Sometimes the burial mounds are made wholly of stones; these are called rock cairns.

The Indians seldom marked the places where they buried their dead. Sometimes plowing or construction activities will expose human bones, showing that a particular spot was used as a burial place. Occasionally a cemetery area can be located by the outline of rock-lined cists or rock-covered graves. Some Indians in almost every period had burial places other than cemeteries, and these generally show up by accident.

The Indians were not really miners, but they did dig rather large holes to obtain the stone that they considered the most suitable for tools and for paint. Flint quarries are generally recognizable as a series of shallow pits with many big chunks of flint at the sides. Paintstone mines are not readily discernible from the surface and have been found in the past when iron ore mines were opened in the central part of the state.

Rock carvings and paintings are much more abundant in Missouri than was realized several years ago. Some of the most outstanding rock carvings or petroglyphs are located at Washington State Park. Many carvings are not easily seen because they have weathered since they were carved. It is suggested that anyone searching for rock carvings first make a trip to Washington State Park to study the petroglyphs which have been preserved there by the Missouri State Park Board. Carvings of thunderbirds, human hands, feet, and ceremonial and fertility symbols are most commonly found. Paintings were usually done in red on cave or shelter walls where the Indians once lived. Most of them have faded badly.

Many different types of Indian sites remain to be found. Most important in making a survey is the exact location of the sites. Carry maps with you on your survey and check all of the features such as houses, roads, streams, hills, and bluffs that will help you place the campsite, cave, mound, or other feature on a map as accurately as possible. A pocket compass is needed so you can orient the map correctly. North is at the top of highway and topographic maps and east is to the right and west to the left. In a notebook or on a printed survey form, available at the Missouri Archaeological Society Survey Office, record a full description of the site including a sketch map, site dimensions, the method used to locate the materials and features, scale used on the sketch map, and, if items are to be collected by units, the size and designation of the units. Do this while on the site and before you pick up the things you plan to collect.

Write the legal description of the site on the form or in the notebook. The legal description is the location of the site within a particular section within a congressional township, which is made up of thirty-six sections numbered from one to thirty-six. Each congressional township is numbered from north to south and from east to west. The east-to-west numbers are called ranges. The township and range numbers locate the particular thirty-six sections within that township and range. Townships are marked on the right and/or left sides of the map, and ranges are marked on the top and bottom of the map. Sections are generally numbered within themselves and are usually one mile square. For the information to be most useful, it is necessary to locate the site within a quarter of quarter of a quarter section, which is within a ten-acre plot. This can be done easily with a pencil by lightly marking off into quarters the particular section where the site is found and then dividing that particular quarter into quarters. The quarters are described by the terms northeast, northwest, southwest, southeast. Thus a site location might be described as "the northeast quarter of the southeast quarter of the northwest quarter of Section 20, Township 34 North, Range 13 West." This is the legal description of a site that makes it possible to find it on a map.

Symbols for site records have been devised and are in use by the Smithsonian Institution, the University of Missouri, and the Missouri Archaeological Society for all sites that are located in Missouri. Perhaps the site that you are planning to record is already located, and a site survey sheet is in the society files at the University of Missouri. If this is the case, you may find out about it by sending the site location to the survey at the University and a site number will be furnished you. The state of Missouri has been given the number symbol 23, as it was the twenty-third in the alphabetical list of the forty-eight states at the time the system was devised. Thus any site located in the state of Missouri would have a number starting with 23. To localize each site further, a symbol has been given for each county in the state. For example, Boone County is given the symbol BO, following the number 23, which indicates the state of Missouri. Each site within the county is then numbered consecutively, starting with 1. Hence, one particular mound in Boone County is numbered 23BO1, a campsite is numbered 23BO2, and so on in the order of their discovery.

The archaeological survey of Missouri is a project conducted cooperatively by the Missouri Archaeological Society and the University of Missouri. A standard form for reporting site locations has been devised. More than twenty-five thousand site locations in Missouri are now reported on these forms and are in the files of the Archaeological Survey. It is estimated that these represent less than 20 percent of the archaeological sites in the state.

In order to work out the prehistory of a particular part of Missouri, it is necessary to know the location of a fair sample of the archaeological sites in the area. Furthermore, it is very important that a sample of the materials be known from each of the locations. When reporting an archaeological site, a complete description of the artifacts from it should accompany the location and description. If possible, photographs of the materials should be attached to the survey sheet. Since this is not always possible, next best is a drawing or sketch of the artifacts, with descriptions. It is very easy to draw artifacts by placing them on a piece of paper, outlining them, and sketching in the major features.

COUNTY SYMBOLS

AD	Adair	GY	Grundy	PY	Perry
AN	Andrews	HA	Harrison	PE	Pettis
AT	Atchison	HE	Henry	PH	Phelps
AU	Audrain	HI	Hickory	PI	Pike
BY	Barry	HO	Holt	PL	Platte
BA	Barton	HD	Howard	PO	Polk
BT	Bates	HL	Howell	PU	Pulaski
BE	Benton	IR	Iron	PT	Putnam
BR	Bollinger	JA	Jackson	RA	Ralls
BO	Boone	JP	Jasper	RN	Randolph
BN	Buchanan	JE	Jefferson	RY	Ray
BU	Butler	JO	Johnson	RE	Reynolds
CW	Caldwell	KN	Knox	RI	Ripley
CY	Callaway	LC	Laclede	SC	St. Charles
CM	Camden	LF	Lafayette	SR	St. Clair
CG	Cape Girardeau	LA	Lawrence	STG	Ste. Genevieve
CA	Carroll	LE	Lewis	SF	St. Francois
CT	Carter	LN	Lincoln	SL	St. Louis
CS	Cass	LI	Linn	SA	Saline
CE	Cedar	LS	Livingston	SK	Schuyler
CH	Chariton	MD	McDonald	SD	Scotland
CN	Christian	MC	Macon	ST	Scott
CK	Clark	MO	Madison	SH	Shannon
CL	Clay	MS	Maries	SY	Shelby
CI	Clinton	MA	Marion	SO	Stoddard
CO	Cole	ME	Mercer	SN	Stone
CP	Cooper	ML	Miller	SU	Sullivan
CR	Crawford	MI	Mississippi	TA	Taney
DA	Dade	MU	Moniteau	TE	Texas
DL	Dallas	MN	Monroe	VE	Vernon
DV	Daviess	MT	Montgomery	WN	Warren
DK	De Kalb	MG	Morgan	WA	Washington
DE	Dent	NM	New Madrid	WE	Wayne
DG	Douglas	NE	Newton	WB	Webster
DU	Dunklin	NO	Nodaway	WO	Worth
FR	Franklin	OR	Oregon	WR	Wright
GA	Gasconade	OS	Osage		
GE	Gentry	OZ	Ozark		
GR	Greene	PM	Pemiscot		

It is almost impossible to overemphasize that very accurate records of the location of archaeological sites and items coming from them must be preserved and studied before the prehistory of any area can be interpreted and described. Site locations and the artifacts found on them—or at least descriptions of them—are basic research materials and as important as historical manuscripts.

If a site is recorded and artifacts are found, the location and the description of the artifacts should be reported to the *Archaeological Survey of Missouri, 15 Switzler Hall, University of Missouri, Columbia, Missouri.* All those who report this information are aiding in the recovery and reconstruction of the prehistory of Missouri and will be credited for their contribution.

Suggested Reading

Alex, Lynn M., 1980. *Exploring Iowa's Past: A Guide to Prehistoric Archaeology*. University of Iowa Press, Iowa City.

American Antiquity. Society for American Archaeology, Washington, D. C.

Fagan, Brian M., 1982. *Archaeology: A Brief Introduction*. Little, Brown and Company, Boston.

Memoir of the Missouri Archaeological Society. Missouri Archaeological Society, Columbia, Missouri.

Midcontinental Journal of Archaeology. The Kent State University Press, Kent, Ohio.

Missouri Archaeological Society Research Series. Columbia, Missouri.

The Missouri Archaeologist. Missouri Archaeological Society, Columbia, Missouri.

Newsletter. Missouri Archaeological Society, Columbia, Missouri.

O'Brien, Michael J., Robert E. Warren, and Dennis E. Lewarch, eds., 1982. *The Cannon Reservoir Human Ecology Project: An Archaeological Study of Cultural Adaptations in the Southern Prairie Peninsula*. Academic Press, New York.

Tools of the Archaeologist

The Archaeologist at Work

Questions that must be answered as part of the preliminary planning are where the site lies in relation to the geography of the locality and to the broad physiographic region, and what its relationships are to other similar sites nearby and within the general region. Just as important is the compilation of all previous information about the site and the cultural materials that are likely to be found. Most pertinent is the preparation of a research design that states explicitly how, when, and why the research is to be conducted and what problem or problems it expects to explore or solve.

The archaeologist studying the early Indian remains in Missouri, unlike the historian, has no written records left by the people to be studied. The remains of camps, villages, houses, tools and utensils (often broken), animal bones, charred vegetables, burial places, earth and stone monuments, and the soil in which the things are encased or making them up must furnish the clues from which the way of life of the people who lived there can be interpreted and written up. The people who are studied have been dead a long time. They were never literate, so all of the history must be interpreted from mute testimony left unintentionally while the people were participating in an ongoing, living culture.

Each archaeological site is like a chapter from the only copy of a rare old history book. There are no other copies, for in the case of the archaeological site, the available information is not exactly the same as in any other site. In a general way the items in the archaeological site are analogous to the words, phrases, and paragraphs on the pages of the only copy of a history book. The arrowheads, pottery vessels, pits, houses, burials, soil color changes, and all the other evidences found in a careful excavation are as important to the interpretation of it as are the words on the pages of a book. The order in which the words are placed in the phrases, the phrases in the sentences, and the sentences in paragraphs on a page makes it possible for one to read the meaning of the words on the page. In the same manner, the association of artifacts with one another and with features such as strata, fireplaces, pits, houses, and burials makes it possible to interpret the story of what happened on the archaeological site. Artifacts alone are like words out of context from the pages of the history book. Both words and artifacts have little to offer in the way of a story unless their proper association is known. Thus, it is extremely important that archaeological excavation be done so carefully, and the association of the artifacts with all of the various features in a site be recorded so well, that the information can be reconstructed on paper and interpreted as a story of the events that took place in the past. Once the site is excavated, all information not recorded or saved is destroyed. If the excavation is not done right the first time, there is no way to go back and correct mistakes.

The tools of the archaeologist are not of a special nature, except those, such as surveying instruments, borrowed from engineering and other fields. The usual complement of excavation tools includes a shovel, a small mattock, a pointing trowel, a limber knife (a grapefruit knife), a whisk broom, a paint brush, a folding rule and steel tape, and—most important—a pencil and record sheets. A surveyor's instruments—an alidade or a transit—are excellent for mapping the site and may be useful for measuring levels in the site as well. A farmer's level, a hand level, or a line level may be used for determining the depths of materials from the surface. A good camera is a necessity, and it is advisable to have a tripod and flash equipment so that pictures can be taken at any time of day or in any situation. It is also desirable and sometimes necessary to take color photos of some of the soil profiles or features where color is important in distinguishing or interpreting the things found. It is almost impossible to have too many pictures of excavations in progress. A good photographic record with full information concerning each picture is extremely helpful in the interpretation of a site. Many times the camera will record items which the excavator overlooked or took for granted. A movie camera that is used to take single frames of each change in an excavation is an inexpensive and reasonable way to record any excavating.

Excavations should not be made by untrained individuals unless they are directed or guided by a trained archaeologist, or unless an emergency—the threatened immediate destruction of the site—is involved. A word to the wise should be sufficient. Before excavating an Indian site, seek the advice of a fully trained archaeologist rather than regret the destruction of our irreplaceable archaeological resources, which is the result of excavation without proper training and knowledge.

Control is the key word of the archaeologist. A controlled excavation is one that is recorded thoroughly as it is being dug. The archaeologist first sets up controls of the horizontal area. This usually involves staking the site into a grid so that all artifacts and evidences can be recorded within it. The grid system in turn is related to permanent objects surrounding the site, such as trees or houses, and these are located on a map to show the exact relationship of the site to the physiographic area. The grid may be set up in feet or meters (meters are preferred), and almost any plan of numbering the grids is acceptable as long as it is understandable to the one doing the excavation and to those reading about it. The system of coordinates using the directions north and east or north and west is one satisfactory method. Excavations are aligned with the cardinal directions or as close to them as is feasible according to the site situation. Coordinates are numbered from hypothetical base lines that are outside the probable limits of the site. One- or two-meter grid squares have been found to be satisfactory in the excavation. If one meter, it is easy to designate the grid lines 101 north, 102 north, 101 east, 102 east, and so on. A particular point on the grid might then read 105N(orth), 109E(ast), and an item located in the grid would be within a one-meter square, between the grid lines 105 north and 109 east, and 106 north and 110 east. To obtain a more exact location, the item can be located within the one-meter square by measuring it from each grid line using centimeters, and its exact location might then read 106.7N, 109.4E, or 7 centimeters north of the 106 north grid line and 4 centimeters east of the 109E grid line.

The second step after setting up the grid is to establish a means of measuring the vertical location from a hypothetical datum line, which is a level line above the site surface from which measurements can be made. The datum line can be established by using a farmer's level, a transit, an alidade, or a surveyor's hand level. The important thing is to establish a base that is a known height above the ground at that point, from which the levels are taken across the site. A stadia rod or any rod marked in meters and centimeters or one marked in feet and inches or tenths of inches can be used to record the depths of the items. The first step is the recording of the

surface of the site from the datum so that actual depths from the surface can be obtained. Similar information can be recorded by setting up stakes at the four corners of the area to be excavated and using a line level to fix a horizontal plane from which all depths are measured.

Once the vertical level or the datum level has been established along the grid for the horizontal area, the basic control of the site excavation has been secured. This is merely the framework of controls within which the archaeologist works, and knowing the framework and how to manipulate it is only the first step in actually doing the digging part of archaeology. Artifacts are only one of the things that need to be recorded in place. More important considerations are the soil context in which they occur and their

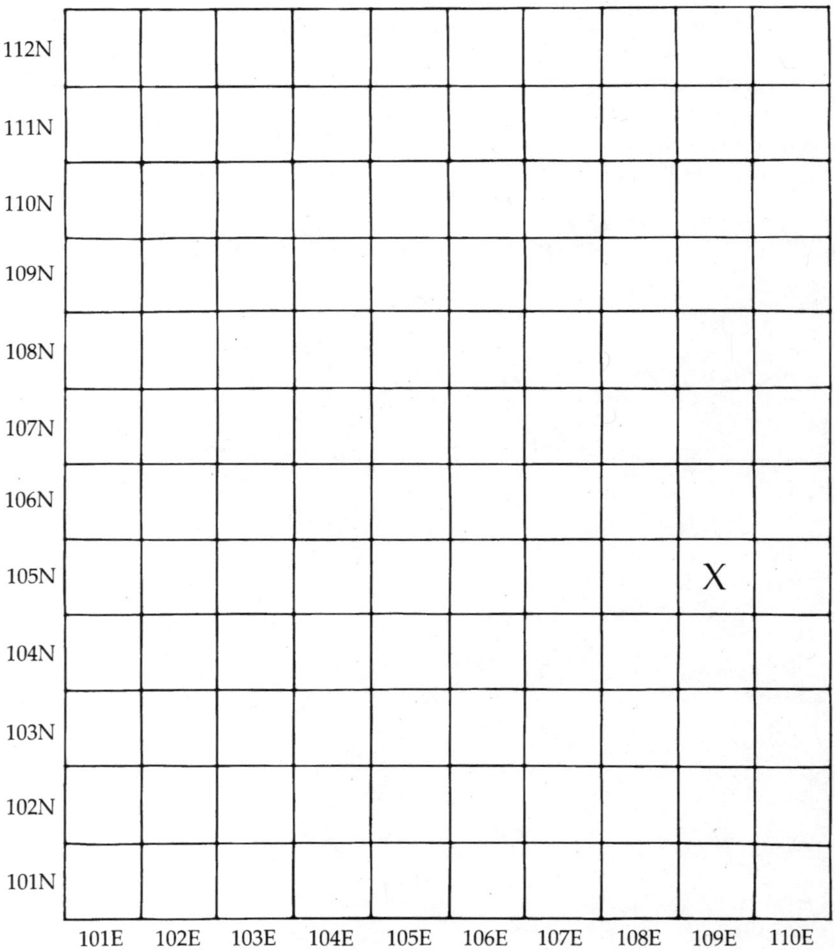

X is grid square 105N 109E

association with features such as fireplaces and pits, house structures, burials, old living surfaces, working areas, and ceremonial places. These are difficult to recognize if one lacks experience and training. A year under the tutelage of an experienced archaeologist is usually considered minimal. To know what to look for, one also needs a general knowledge of Indian cultures. Archaeologists must have a long period of training in which to obtain a thorough background of information concerning the Indian cultures as well as previous archaeological work done in the area and the region. This knowledge must be at one's finger tips so that it can be related to the planning and direction of the excavation of any particular site.

The excavation of a campsite or village site is usually a big undertaking. The reason for digging the site is not just to obtain a selection of the tools and implements which the people made, but also to gain a thorough description of the types of shelters they built, the pits or storage houses they constructed for preserving foods and material, and the relationship of these structures to other houses, pits, and features in the entire living area. Excavations should be guided so that enough detailed information is obtained from a house structure that its utilization by the people and their social relationships can be interpreted. This would include data about sleeping areas, storage places, and working sections and their use by people of different ages and sexes and by different social units, if more

Mapping the Site

than one social unit occupied a house. The position of the house in regard to other houses may give an insight to the social-political structure of the village. In order to gain this knowledge, a series of houses needs to be excavated on the village site. Houses should be noted in relation to plazas, and to defensive or protective embankments or ditches surrounding the village, if they are present, or to natural features such as river banks. The actual digging of the campsite or village site is only the beginning of the labor involved in a good archaeological excavation, as the information recovered should be so exact, so complete, that the site can be reconstructed on paper in the laboratory.

Vertical profiles are needed to show house floors or a series of occupations in a site. Horizontal profiles are necessary to find pits or postmolds in their proper relationships. For example, postmolds often define the walls and supports of a house. A horizontal profile may also show up fireplaces and evidences of other structures such as smudge pits.

The excavations of caves and shelters are similar to the excavations of campsites, with the exception that the materials are concentrated in a smaller area and usually have undergone more disturbance from the human inhabitants and animals. In the case of cave excavations, it is extremely important to make sure that all disturbances are noted and that all materials in association with them are recorded. Caves that were occupied for a long time are extremely difficult to record and interpret, and a

House Outlined by Postmolds

person who excavates a cave or shelter site should have several years of training before attempting this type of investigation.

Sometimes a shelter is so dry that it is difficult to use normal procedures of cutting vertical and horizontal profiles, and other methods must be devised. The occasional occurrence of perishable materials necessitates more careful work and special means of preservation. Ordinary excavation techniques can destroy fragile, perishable objects.

All investigations should involve the taking of soil samples for pollen and chemical analyses and for flotation to obtain charred vegetal remains and microfauna such as small fish and mammal bones. Animal and vegetable remains should be preserved until they can identified and reported upon by ethnobiologists. Charcoal may be useful for radiocarbon dating. The charcoal must be associated with the particular complex or group of artifacts in a specific occupational level in a site before it is valuable for dating purposes. Charcoal unaccompanied by thorough records concerning its location and association with the artifacts and other features in the site is worthless.

Mound excavations call for special techniques and methods, depending upon the type of mound and upon the area in which it is located. Many mounds have interior rock structures that were built as chambers for the

Vertical Profile, Graham Cave

entombment of the dead. A trench cut through a mound of this type would destroy a part of the structure, and might make it difficult to record. Where an interior structure exists, enough of it should be uncovered first to determine its structure. In mounds where there are no structures, trenching into them is a desirable technique. A trench through one side of the mound to its center and a carefully cut profile should furnish good clues to the mound construction. Mounds are evidence of a part of the ceremonial life of the Indians and must be viewed in this context. The investigation of a mound should be on the basis of attempting to reconstruct the ceremony or to ascertain any other reason for building it.

The excavation of burials should not be a hunt for grave goods. Many Indians did not bury artifacts with their dead, and in any instance, the artifacts themselves without the information concerning the burial are of little historical or anthropological value. The proper excavation of burials necessitates a knowledge of physical anthropology—the anatomy of the human body. Measurements of the skeleton should be made while it is in place to determine the height, sex, and age of the individual. In order to do

Cutting a Horizontal Profile

Rock Structure in a Burial Mound

Earth Mound Excavation

this, all bones must be uncovered very carefully and left undisturbed until measurements are made. Furthermore, the skeleton needs to be photographed before it is removed. All bones of the skeleton should be saved, and the right side kept separate from the left. It is advisable to make the bones available to a physical anthropologist for further study of any abnormality or pathology that they might reveal. Data about diet might also be determined through chemical analysis. Samples of the soil in which the burial was encased should also be saved for chemical and phytological analyses.

Although the position of the skeleton and the materials buried with the individual are important, perhaps more pertinent is the relationship of the burial to other burials within the cemetery area. It is from this kind of evidence that interpretations can be made concerning the use of the cemetery areas by families, clans, or other social or political groups. Only through this additional information is it possible to gain a picture of the people as they lived, believed, practiced their customs, and died.

Last and most important is a fully written report, ready for publication, describing and interpreting the archaeological sites that have been dug. If the knowledge obtained from an excavation is never made available for others to read, evaluate, and use, the excavation has been destructive rather than helpful.

The preceding has been a brief sketch of some of the procedures used in the different types of excavations that the archaeologist conducts; it is certainly not detailed enough to be used as a guide for proper methodology. It is recommended that no excavation be attempted by any individual who has not had thorough training and the experience of working with trained archaeologists. If emergency salvage of an archaeological site is needed, consult a professional archaeologist for help and advice.

The survey for archaeological sites is the place to begin if you are interested in archaeology and want to be an amateur archaeologist. The location of sites, the collection of artifacts, and the keeping of proper records are very much needed. Before digging, an individual should first learn how to control the data on a limited basis by working with professional archaeologists. Advice from the trained archaeologist should be the guide from there on. Do not destroy the past; help preserve and interpret it.

Students who are interested in making archaeology a career should, in their high school training, get a well-rounded education with emphasis upon social, biological, and natural sciences, for example, geology, chemistry, mathematics, biology, botany, geography, history, sociology, and anthropology. The archaeologist must have a familiarity with the historical and cultural development of the people who left the remains. The capable archaeologist must be able to draw upon special techniques from many sciences as aids in order to show the relationship of early mankind to the natural and cultural environment.

Members of the Missouri Archaeological Society cooperating with University of Missouri staff archaeologists in the excavation of an Oneota village site. The Missouri Archaeological Society has aided the University of Missouri in the investigation of many of the sites that form the basis for the interpretation of the prehistory of Missouri.

Suggested Reading

Brothwell, Don, and Eric Higgs, eds., 1963. *Science in Archaeology*. Basic Books, New York.

Butzer, Karl W., 1982. *Archeology as Human Ecology*. Cambridge University Press, New York.

Fagan, Brian M., 1983. *Archaeology: A Brief Introduction*. 2d ed., Little, Brown and Company, Boston.

Green, Ernestine L., 1973. *In Search of Man: Readings in Archaeology*. Little, Brown and Company, Boston.

Hester, Thomas R., Robert F. Heizer, and John A. Graham, 1975. *Field Methods in Archaeology*. 6th ed., Mayfield Publishing Company, Palo Alto, California.

Joukowsky, Martha, 1980. *A Complete Manual of Field Archaeology: Tools and Techniques of Field Work for Archaeologists*. Prentice-Hall, Inc., Englewood Cliffs, New Jersey.

McGimsey, Charles R., III, and Hester A. Davis, 1977. *The Management of Archeological Resources: The Airlie House Report*. Society for American Archaeology, Washington, D.C.

MacNeish, Richard S., 1978. *The Science of Archaeology?* Duxbury Press, North Scituate, Massachusetts.

Rouse, Irving, 1972. *Introduction to Prehistory: A Systematic Approach*. McGraw-Hill, Inc., New York.

Stuart, George E., 1976. *Your Career in Archaeology*. Society for American Archaeology, Washington, D.C.

Looking to the Future

"There is nothing new under the sun"—is an old adage that holds a great deal of truth. Anything new is immediately old, so to speak, for it is in the past by the time it is observed, recorded, and considered. If an event has happened, it is in the past. It is amazing how important the past is to us and how dependent we are upon it. For example, imagine the chaos if all of us were suddenly to have amnesia. No one would know how to run complicated machinery or how to carry on the duties of everyday living. Our whole civilization would collapse. But what has this to do with digging up Indian remains?

Today we know more about atoms and atomic power than we know about mankind. Our technology has progressed so far and so fast that it is even possible for us to destroy our world, and this control of the physical world threatens to be used for destructive purposes. Do we know enough about ourselves to control these destructive forces and put them to useful purposes? Can we predict the future? Is it possible to have a hand in guiding it? The answer fortunately is "Yes," but we must go to the past if we are to predict events that are to come. We must know our past if we are to help guide our future. We must know as much as possible about the human ways of living we have inherited; it is absolutely necessary to push forward the study of mankind and culture in every way feasible and as fast as we can.

Prediction is nothing new, and we continue to project our predictions, based upon the past, further and further into the future. All of us make appointments with the dentist, the doctor, and business associates; we plan trips, use a calendar, a train schedule, a plane schedule, or an appointment book. We predict with a great deal of accuracy many of our activities quite far in advance of the event.

But what has this to do with archaeology and Indians? Our own culture, our civilization, is so complex and we are so involved in it, unconsciously as well as consciously, that we have difficulty in looking at it objectively to see how and why it works. If we turn to the Indians and to the past, we can look at less complicated ways of living, and as we are not involved in that way of living, we can look at it more objectively. We can more readily see the whys and wherefores of it. Studying relatively simple cultures and following their development through time furnishes students of social science with a laboratory for cultural study and allows them to develop hypotheses and theories that can then be applied to the more complex problems of the modern world for better understanding of our present culture. In other words, the study of archaeology and Indians in the Americas or excavating Indian remains can contribute to the knowledge of the factors that cause civilzations to come into being, flourish, and then decline.

There are further benefits to be derived from the study of American Indians and their cultures, for a great part of our present-day American heritage stems directly from the Indians. The field of study of American archaeology is relatively new and is still in the process of developing techniques and methods of reaching into the past. It has the role of putting flesh on the skeleton of the past and making it live again. It allows us to gain insights about the development of another culture that might be applied to our own. It should aid in understanding more about ourselves, where we have been, and where we are going.

The historical knowledge about Missouri is very limited. Slightly more than three hundred years ago, in 1673, we have the first limited information from the brief notes of Marquette and Jolliet. Missouri became a state in 1821, less than two centuries ago. At that time Indians were still living in the state and had reservation lands within it. Compare this with the more than ten thousand years of Indian occupation of Missouri preceding A.D. 1673. This is the storehouse of knowledge, still virtually untapped, which can form a vast laboratory for the study of human ways of living and how they are affected by climate, drought, floods, and other aspects of the environment.

Furthermore, many different Indian tribes met in what is now Missouri, and it is possible to learn much from these encounters concerning what happens when two groups of people with different ideas and different backgrounds come together. It is even possible to see the effects of potentially destructive inventions such as the bow and arrow, which was as greatly advanced a weapon in Missouri at approximately A.D. 800 as the atomic bomb is in our own time.

It is not proposed that American archaeology will immediately furnish tremendous or spectacular advances of knowledge to straighten out world problems or even to affect the trend of events in the world in the near future. It is expected, nevertheless, that solid information leading to the understanding of human ways of life will be derived from the studies. At the very least the comprehension of the past of all mankind will be enriched with a greater knowledge of the people who preceded us in Missouri and in North America.

Important areas of knowledge are climatic changes, vegetation changes, soil changes, changes in animal life, and the utilization and destruction of these resources through the human existence on earth. Knowledge of local environmental effects such as flood and drought cycles may be essential to the planning of our modern use of such areas. All of these things are recorded in the campsites and other places occupied and utilized by the Indians.

Human skeletal material holds practical value for dentists and doctors and for physical anthropologists studying anatomy, growth, and nutrition. The knowledge of the use in the past of medicinal plants and the cultivation of native food plants may be beneficial to an overpopulated world in the future. We must go to the past through archaeological research to find out what these cultural-historical-environmental resources are before they are destroyed by the onslaught of our present-day civilization. The construction of dams, roads, and factories and the expansion of our cities and our farming operations are rapidly depleting archaeological sites throughout the United States.

In Missouri a broad program of archaeological research was begun by the University of Missouri and the Missouri Archaeological Society in the 1930s. The greatest emphasis has been upon the salvage of information from the reservoir areas where dams were being built for flood control, power, and water conservation. The work has been done in cooperation with the National Park Service and has yielded information that otherwise would now be lost beneath the backwaters of the dams. In the past few years, the U.S. Corps of Engineers has supported projects in the Truman and Cannon reservoirs. In each instance where research has been conducted, a mass of new data has been retrieved that reveals and broadens the knowledge of the past in that particular segment of the world.

At the same time that research has been concentrated in the reservoir areas, a full program of archaeological research has been in operation throughout the state. The archaeological survey of Missouri has been continued by the Missouri Archaeological Society, working with the American Archaeology division, Anthropology Department, College of Arts and Science, University of Missouri–Columbia. A program was also developed in cooperation with the Missouri State Park Board and the University of Missouri to recover, preserve, interpret, and display the archaeological finds in the state parks. Archaeological research has also been conducted in different parts of the state in an attempt to salvage sites that have been threatened with destruction and to investigate key sites and areas that might furnish important additional contributions to the knowledge of Missouri's past. The Missouri State Highway Department has aided in rescuing information from numerous archaeological sites that would have been damaged or destroyed by the construction of federal and state highways, and through advance planning has avoided the destruction of many sites by routing highways around them. Special projects have been supported by private organizations such as the Lucy Wortham James Foundation and the Duenke Construction Company. Problem-oriented research on Osage and Missouri Indian prehistory and on Rodgers Shelter, Hopewell, Oneota, and Mississippian settlement systems has been conducted with the aid of National Science Foundation and National Endowment for the Humanities grants.

Other universities in Missouri such as the University of Missouri–St.

Louis, Southwest Missouri State University (Springfield), Southeast Missouri State University (Cape Girardeau), Central Missouri State University (Warrensburg), Northeast Missouri State University (Kirksville), Northwest Missouri State University (Maryville), and Washington University (St. Louis) have carried out archaeological work in the state. Institutions from other states including the University of Arkansas, University of Kansas, Kansas State University, University of Arizona, University of Nebraska, University of Michigan, Memphis State University, Luther College (Iowa), and the Illinois State Museum have been active in archaeological work in Missouri. All have added to the overall knowledge of Missouri's past. It is through these many and varied phases of archaeological research that the knowledge of Missouri prehistory, skeletal a half century ago, has had flesh added to its bare bones. The prehistory of the state is no longer a speculative mystery. It is a coherent though incomplete picture of the adjustment of one branch of mankind, the Indians, to the natural and cultural environment for twelve thousand years or more in one portion of the world, the state of Missouri.

Historians and anthropologists believe that mankind's past experience is needed as a guide to the future. Humans have lived on the earth so long that it is difficult to comprehend the length of time involved. A rough estimate in the form of an analogy is that mankind's average life span compares to much less than an hour in a year, if a year would represent the total time of human existence on earth. People have adapted their modes of life to all types of environments and living conditions. They have experimented successfully and unsuccessfully with plants, animals, and land use. Many of these experiments and their results have been lost to our present knowledge, but the keys to them still exist in the ruins of past campsites, towns, and cities, the remnants of past cultures and civilizations. They can be made available to us if the evidences of them are not destroyed before they are rediscovered through careful archaeological research.

The future is based on the past, and we cannot say what will be important for us to know tomorrow or in the distant future. Therefore, it behooves us to obtain all the information possible about the past. Those who follow us in the future might have need of it.

Glossary

adz
a cutting tool with the plane of the blade set at right angles to the handle. It is considered to be a woodworking tool and is usually made of flint.

aggregate
the sum total of materials occurring on an archaeological site.

antediluvian
before the Deluge, the great flood referred to in the Bible.

anthropology
the study of mankind and human culture.

archaeology
a series of techniques, methodology, and theory designed to reconstruct and interpret past culture.

arrowhead
a small projectile point often less than one and one-half inches in length, used to tip an arrowshaft.

arrowshaft straightener
a bone or antler with a hole in it through which an arrowshaft was inserted to determine, by sighting along its length, whether it needed straightening; if so, this tool was used to wrench the arrowshaft into shape.

artifacts
a general term for tools, weapons, utensils, and other items made by human beings.

assemblage
a group of artifacts seeming to belong to a single culture.

atlatl
a spear thrower, a device that makes it possible to throw a spear farther and with greater speed than with the arm only.

awl
a pointed bone or antler tool used either in the manufacture of skin items and clothing or in weaving.

Aztalan
the site of a Mississippi period fortified village in Jefferson County, Wisconsin.

Black Sand phase (focus)
an Early Woodland period cultural unit first described in Illinois. Sand-tempered pottery, with incised decoration over the cord making, is diagnostic of the phase.

bola
a throwing weapon consisting of weights made of baked clay, stone, or bone attached to the ends of thongs or cords.

Burkett Site
an Early Woodland period site in Mississippi County, Missouri.

cache pit
a hole dug in the ground in which articles of value were stored or hidden

while the Indians were away on hunting trips.

Caddo tribe
: refers to the Kadohadacho Confederacy belonging to the Caddo division of the Caddoan linguistic stock. The Kadohadacho lived in northeastern Texas and southwestern Arkansas at the Great Bend of Red River.

Cahokia site
: the large mound group and village site area in the American Bottom, East St. Louis, Illinois. Some of the mounds, including the largest in the group, Monks Mound, are preserved in a state park.

Cahokia tribe
: one of the Illinois tribes of Indians who were living in the state of Illinois in the early part of the historic period.

campsite
: an open area used for camping. Flint spalls and broken tools are usual evidences of a campsite.

Chiwere
: a Siouan language division that includes the Winnebago, Oto, Iowa, and Missouri tribes.

clan
: a social unit, the members of which are assumed to be descended from a common ancestor who is often symbolized by some type of mythical figure. If the clan is patrilineal the individual belongs to the father's clan, if matrilineal the individual obtains membership through the mother. Individuals usually must marry outside their clan membership.

cord marking
: a pottery decoration produced by pressing the vessel surface with a cord-wrapped tool when the clay is still plastic or malleable.

cultural area
: a geographic area within which the cultures of various societies are similar.

culture
: the lifeways of a particular people, including the habits, customs, and artifacts associated with gaining their living, organizing their social and political activities, and practicing their religious rituals and ceremonies.

cupstone
: a rock, usually sandstone, which has one or more depressions pecked or ground into its surface. The cups or depressions are often less than an inch in diameter and less than one-half inch deep.

Delaware tribe
: Indians from the eastern part of the United States, some of whom moved to Missouri in 1789 and held reservation lands in the state until 1829.

dentate stamping
: a decorative motif on pottery vessels, impressed with a toothed comblike tool while the clay is still plastic or malleable.

discoidal
: a polished stone object, usually biconcave, occasionally biconvex or perforated, considered to be associated with a game called chunkey, which was

played in historic times in the southeastern part of the United States.

disk pipe

a variety of pipe in which the lip of the bowl is flattened out widely, giving it the appearance of a disk.

ear-spool

a spool-shaped object usually made of stone, inserted through or attached to the earlobe for ornamentation.

ethnography

the descriptive study of the cultural characteristics of diverse human societies, especially in reference to primitive nonliterate people.

ethnology

the study of culture on a comparative and theoretical basis.

evolution (cultural)

the change of culture or formal cultural units through time through innovative, adaptive means.

exogamy

proscribed marriage outside the social unit or local group.

fish gorge

a double-pointed piece of bone or stone attached midway between the two sharp points to a fishing line to serve as a fishhook.

flake knife

a long, thin flake of flint that either is unmodified or has fine chipping on the edges only.

flake scraper

a flake of flint that has been snubbed off on one end to be used for scraping purposes. They are sometimes called end scrapers, snub-nosed or snubbed-end flake scrapers.

flesher (leg bone)

a type of scraper for removing bits of flesh and fat from skins in preparation for their use as clothing or other articles.

flint

a cryptocrystalline stone that breaks with a conchoidal fracture and can be shaped easily into artifacts by flaking and chipping techniques. Geologists often consider only the dark gray or black varieties of this stone to be flint and call the lighter varieties chert and the translucent variety chalcedony. The term *flint* was first applied to all chert or flint stones flaked into tools, and logically it is retained today.

fluted points

projectile points with a groove or grooves down the center of the blade. The groove is made by the removal of one or more large flakes from the base.

focus

(*see* phase)

Fox tribe

(*see* Sauk and Fox)

galena

native lead occurring in cuboidal form and often used by the Indians without much alteration.

gorget
a relatively large ornament perforated in one or more places for suspension and worn at the throat or chest.

graver
a sharp-pointed cutting or engraving tool usually made of flint.

grit tempering
crushed particles of rock such as limestone, chert, or granite which are added intentionally to pottery clay. The grit tempering is supposed to keep the pottery vessel from breaking when it is fired.

hachuring
a type of pottery decoration consisting of filling or decorating an area with a series of parallel incised or trailed lines.

hammerstone
usually an unmodified pebble used as a hammer.

horizontal profile
in excavation procedure, the smoothed, cleaned horizontal surface.

horticulture
the cultivation of domesticated plants by the use of a hoe or a digging stick.

Illinois tribes
a group of Algonquian-speaking Indian tribes sometimes known as the Illinois Confederacy, usually including the Cahokia, Kaskaskia, Michigamea, Moingwena, Peoria, and Tamaroa.

incising
a type of pottery decoration in which lines of a design are drawn with a sharp instrument, producing a narrow or V-shaped cut on the malleable or plastic surface of the pottery vessel.

Iowa tribe
one of the Chiwere group of Siouan-speaking Indians who lived in the general area of the present state of Iowa, which was named for them.

Jakie Shelter
a large shelter in the Table Rock Reservoir area of Barry County in southwestern Missouri. It had been utilized by the Indians for about seven thousand years. Excavation of the shelter deposits provided much information on the archaeological sequence in the area.

Kansas tribe
one of the Dhegiha group of Siouan-speaking Indians closely related to the Osage, Omaha, Ponca, and Quapaw. They lived along the Kansas River. The state and river were named after the Kansas tribe.

Kaskaskia tribe
one of the Illinois tribes that lived part of the time on the west side of the Mississippi River near St. Louis.

Kickapoo tribe
a group of Algonquian-speaking Indians closely related to the Sauk and Fox, originally living in Ohio, Michigan, Indiana, and Illinois. They came to Missouri in 1819 and had a reservation in the western part of the state until they moved to Kansas.

lanceolate (projectile point or knife)
an unnotched blade with maximum width through the middle and tapering toward both the base and the point. It is a type of chipped stone artifact that is similar to the metal lance points of the historic period.

Lehner Site
a mammoth-kill site in Arizona at which Clovis Fluted points were found associated with extinct elephant bones.

Little Osage tribe
a portion of the Osage Indian tribe that moved to central Missouri in the early part of the eighteenth century and remained there until the latter part of the century, when they returned to their old homeland along the Osage River in southwestern Missouri.

mammoth
an extinct type of elephant, a grazing animal that lived in grasslands.

mano
a hand stone that has been shaped for use as a grinding or mealing stone in connection with a metate. It is used for crushing and grinding seeds.

marmiton
an Osage town crier and chief cook, one of the prominent personages in the village. Also the name of a branch of the Osage River.

mastodon
an extinct type of elephant that lived in forested regions as well as in grasslands. It ate leaves, twigs, grasses, and the tender parts of trees and shrubs.

Maya
Indians living in the peninsula of Yucatan, Mexico, and in the surrounding area, whose ancestors were the scientists of the New World. They developed mathematics and astronomy to a high degree and had a form of writing.

metate
a flat stone upon which seeds and other foods are mashed and ground. A hand stone or mano is used with it.

Modoc Shelter
an Archaic period site in Illinois which yielded a sequence of cultural items and a series of radiocarbon dates. It was excavated by the Illinois State Museum.

moiety
a dual division of a tribe, band, or society, usually for the purpose of regulating marriage and conducting ceremonies.

Mound City
the name sometimes applied to St. Louis, which was the site of a large group of mounds until the early nineteenth century.

Naco Site
a mammoth-kill site in Arizona at which Clovis Fluted points were found associated with mammoth bones.

Neosho focus (phase)
a relatively late archaeological unit in northeastern Oklahoma. It appears

to be related both to the Oneota and the earlier Mississippi period cultures.

Omaha tribe
a Dhegiha Siouan-speaking tribe originally located in Nebraska near the present city of Omaha. They were closely related to the Ponca, Osage, Kansas, and Quapaw.

Oneota
a broad cultural grouping in the north central Mississippi–lower Missouri river region. The Winnebago, Iowa, Missouri, Oto, and Osage have been identified with the archaeological Oneota culture.

Oto tribe
an Indian tribe originally living in Nebraska. They were Chiwere Siouan-speaking people with whom the Missouri Indian tribe amalgamated after A.D. 1800.

Paleo-Indian
the archaeological period from about 12,000 to 8000 B.C. Big-game hunting is one of the characteristics of the period.

Paleolithic
the Old Stone Age in the Old World. It equates with the Early Hunter period in the Americas.

palette
a thin piece of stone, usually sandstone, used for mixing paint. It may also have been a tool for polishing or grinding stone objects. Sandstone palettes often have evidences of red ocher or hematite paint clinging to them.

Pawnee tribe
one of the principal tribes of the Caddoan linguistic stock. They lived on the middle course of the Platte River and the Republican Fork of the Kansas River.

Peoria tribe
one of the Illinois Confederacy.

pestle
an unmodified river pebble that has been used for grinding seeds and other foods in a mortar. Sometimes pestles were pecked and ground into cylindrical or bell shapes.

phase
an archaeological cultural unit that is sufficiently uniform and distinctive to separate it from other units. It must also have reasonably discrete spatial and chronological boundaries.

phratry
two or more clans that form a social grouping within a tribe.

physiographic area
a geographic area in which the fauna, flora, and topography are similar.

physiography
the physical geography or topography of an area.

Piankashaw
a band of the Miami tribe that had a village in southwestern Missouri for a short time.

Pleistocene
the last period of the Cenozoic. It is generally called the Ice Age, as glaciation was characteristic of the period.

plummet
a stone shaped like a plumbob or a tear drop, with a groove around the tapering end or a hole through if for suspension. These stones were probably bola stones (*see* bola).

postmold
the evidence in the ground of a house post or any wooden post after the wood has rotted away. It is identifiable by the darker color in the soil or a cavity.

potsherd
a piece of a broken pottery vessel.

Poverty Point
a cultural unit of the Late Archaic, possibly occurring in the bootheel area of southeastern Missouri.

protohistoric
the time immediately preceding the beginning of written history in an area. Quite often European trade goods occur on protohistoric sites, since trade items found their way to the Indians before there was any written history concerning them.

Pueblo Indians
Indians living in compact permanent settlements in the southwestern part of the United States, i.e., Arizona and New Mexico. The Indian towns are built of adobe and stone and often are apartment buildings several stories high.

Quapaw tribe
one of the Dhegiha Siouan linguistic group, closely related to the Osage, Omaha, Kansas, and Ponca. They lived in several villages near the mouth of the Arkansas River in the present state of Arkansas. Another name for them is Arkansas, and the name of the river and the state was derived from this tribe.

radiocarbon dating
a method of obtaining the date of bone, shell, or vegetable items by measuring the amount of radioactivity of carbon 14 in them.

Rice Shelter
an important site in Stone County, Missouri, in the Table Rock Reservoir area. It yielded information about the early people that lived in the region. It is a type site for several projectile points.

riverine
referring to river valleys and the things closely associated with the river valleys.

Sauk (Sac) and Fox tribe
originally two separate tribes speaking the Algonquian language. By the time they moved to the northeastern part of Missouri they had amalgamated.

secondary burial
the burial of human bones after the flesh has been removed. Sometimes

the flesh was removed intentionally after the bodies had been exposed on a scaffold or had been buried temporarily elsewhere. Usually the bones were collected and reburied after the flesh had decayed.

shamans
magico-religious functionaries whose main activities were to heal the sick or to perform magical rites for the good of individuals or the society. They were usually mediators between the mundane and the spirit world.

Shawnee tribe
Indians who came from the Tennessee Valley area. Part of the tribe migrated to Missouri along with the Delaware in 1789. They had reservations in the eastern and southwestern parts of the state and had villages on the Bourbeuse River and Apple, Shawnee, and Huzzah creeks.

shell tempering
small pieces of crushed shell added to the clay before making pottery.

site
any localized evidences left by the Indians such as a camping place, a burial mound, or a ceremonial place.

spear thrower
a board or stick with a hook at one end for the attachment of the nock end of a dart or spear (*see* atlatl).

spindle whorl
the perforated clay or stone disk attached to a spindle, used in the preparation of yarn for weaving.

spud
a celt-shaped polished stone artifact with flaring bit, perhaps having a ceremonial purpose.

tallies
bone or wooden objects, with lines cut or painted on them, which are used for making counts or keeping scores.

tempering
any substance such as crushed shell, crushed grit, or sand added to pottery clay in order to prevent cracking when the vessel is fired.

tinklers
conical thin metal objects used as freely hanging decorations on clothing and spaced closely enough that movement causes them to produce a tinkling sound.

town crier
(*see* marmiton)

trailed lines
lines drawn with a round-ended or a dull instrument on pottery that is still malleable or plastic. The lines are usually U-shaped in cross-section.

trait (cultural)
a single element or item that is considered to be part of a particular culture. It may be an artifact, house structure, pit, or any smallest unit of a cultural manifestation.

use polish
the polish produced by the use of a tool or utensil, such as the polish on a spade or scraper.

vertical profile
in archaeological techniques, the smoothly cut vertical plane of an excavation in the soil.

wattle and daub
house wall construction consisting of a framework of vertical posts interlaced horizontally with canes or tree branches (the wattle) and plastered with clay (the daub).

Wea
a subdivision or band of the Miami tribe that was located for a short time in southwestern Missouri.

Winnebago tribe
one of the Chiwere Siouan-speaking Indian tribes, closely related to the Iowa, Missouri, and Oto. They lived on the shore of Lake Winnebago in Wisconsin.

About the Authors

Carl H. Chapman was Professor of Anthropology and Research Professor in American Archaeology at the University of Missouri–Columbia until his and Eleanor's untimely deaths in an automobile accident in 1987. He was the author of *The Archaeology of Missouri* and *Osage Indians III: The Origin of the Osage Indian Tribe,* as well as numerous articles in scholarly journals and chapters of books.

Eleanor F. Chapman held a college degree in art and had illustrated archaeological publications since 1946. She was Art Editor of the *Missouri Archaeologist,* the journal of the Missouri Archaeological Society, until 1962, at which time she was given a Special Award of Appreciation by the Society. She was also Art Editor of the Society Memoir series. She was coauthor with Henry and Jean Hamilton of *Spiro Mound Copper* as well as the illustrator of *The Archaeology of Missouri* and of many articles in scientific journals and chapters in books.